HOW TO FIGHT
PRESIDENTS

HOW TO
FIGHT
PRESIDENTS

DEFENDING YOURSELF AGAINST THE
BADASSES WHO RAN THIS COUNTRY

★ ★ ★

DANIEL O'BRIEN

ILLUSTRATED BY WINSTON ROWNTREE

THREE RIVERS PRESS
NEW YORK

Published in the United States by Three Rivers Press,
an imprint of the Crown Publishing Group,
a division of Random House LLC,
a Penguin Random House Company, New York.
www.crownpublishing.com

Three Rivers Press and the Tugboat design
are registered trademarks of Random House LLC.

Library of Congress Cataloging-in-Publication data is available upon request.

ISBN 978-0-385-34757-0
eBook ISBN 978-0-385-34758-7

Printed in the United States of America

Book design by Jaclyn Reyes
Illustrations by Winston Rowntree
Cover design by Michael Nagin
Cover photography by Michael S. Heath

1 3 5 7 9 10 8 6 4 2

First Edition

This book is dedicated to my father,
who is more badass than any of the presidents in this book,
and my mother, who is smarter and sweeter.
For Tommy and David.
And for Elise.

CONTENTS

★ ★ ★

"It took a lot of blood, sweat, and tears to get where we are today, but we have just begun."

–BARACK OBAMA (a president)

HOW TO FIGHT
PRESIDENTS

INTRODUCTION

YOU'D HAVE TO BE CRAZY

TO WANT THIS JOB

★ ★ ★

I look out at all of the fresh young faces in this classroom and I can think of one thing to say: not one of you is ever going to grow up to be the president of the United States."

That was the very first thing my American Government professor said on the very first day of class in my freshman year at Rowan University. He didn't say it to get a laugh, and in fact glared at anyone who so much as smirked. I know, because *I* smirked, and I was wearing pajama pants at the time, and that was another thing he hated (I maintained that I was honoring the spirit of the class by declaring very comfortable independence from my constricting oppressors [buttons and zippers], but he refused to be swayed). He went on to say that he had worked long enough at this university that he was technically un-fireable, and since absolutely nothing could touch his job security, being well-liked was not important to him. His stated goal was not to teach us about American Government ("a fool's errand," he called it), nor was it to prepare us for a life *in* government ("Get over yourself"). His only ambition was to spend the next semester getting us "mentally equipped enough to properly read the newspaper, but honestly I don't even think most of you could handle that. Especially not you, in the pajama pants, in public, during the day, god*dammit* come on, are those women's pants? You are a boy."

Out of every crotchety insult he delivered in his opening lecture (and every crotchety insult he would aim at me throughout the semester, including use of the persistent nickname "PJ Pete," a frankly unfair label for someone who wore pajamas *one time* and was, in fact, named Daniel), the only thing that really stuck with me was his first accusation: that I would never be president.

I never wanted to be president, but when that constantly angry professor told me I couldn't—*even if I wanted to*—something inside of me was triggered and I thought, "Oh yeah? I'll show you. I'm going to be president. I'm going to be president *all over* this country, and there's not a damn thing you can do about it."

See, I have a deep-seated problem with authority that has instilled in me a drive to immediately do whatever it is a powerful person says I can't do. I also have an even *deeper*-seated desire to be a giant nerd, so this particular act of rebellion took the form of me going to the university library to read absolutely everything I could about presidents. When trying to get back at a teacher, some students will key a car or throw toilet paper at a house. I attacked books with a similar amount of gusto and, no, I *didn't* think there was anything weird about this (and, no, I *didn't* get invited to a lot of parties).

I consumed everything I could. Biographies, autobiographies. The journal of John Quincy Adams. The financial records of George Washington. The private letters of Warren G. Harding. Pictures of JFK in a swimsuit. All of it. I was trying to crack a code. I was looking for similarities between not just our greatest presidents, but *all* of our presidents. At the time, only forty-two guys in history had ever taken the job. There must have been *some* trait they all shared, some common bond, some characteristic that linked every president across two hundred and some-odd years. Something I could study, master, and apply to myself so that I too could one day be president. Not to help the country in any way, just so I could shove it in my professor's face and then quickly resign. It turns out there *was* one thing I learned in my exhaustive study of all things presidential:

You'd have to be crazy to want this job.

I don't mean to be casual about that; I mean that the desire to be the president is a currently undiagnosed but very specific form of insanity. Only a person with an unfathomably huge ego and an off-the-charts level of blind self-confidence and an insatiable hunger for control could look at America, in all of her enormity, with all of her complexity, with all of her beauty and flaws and strength and power, and say, "Yeah. *I* should be in charge of that." Only a lunatic would look at a job where you get slandered and scrutinized and attacked by the media and sometimes even assassinated and say, "Sign me up!" Only a lunatic.

I learned that my professor was right. I didn't have the specific version of crazy required to be the president. But I *also* learned that presidents, with all of their madness and passion and recklessness and acts of desperation in their relentless quest to become America's king, were interesting and wild and *freaking badass*. They had balls, and their balls had balls. They were *tough*.

I was so fascinated with the nutcases we made president that I never stopped reading about them, even after that American Government class ended, but my studies took on a different tone. Knowing that I didn't have what it took to be president, I started thinking about what it would take to *defeat* a president, mentally or physically, via psychological warfare or . . . the warfare kind of warfare. I looked at the club of presidents and put a spin on the old adage: If you can't join them, *beat them*.

That's what you're reading right now. The most interesting, exciting, bizarre, or otherwise badass facts about every great psychopath who has ever stood on top of Mount America and declared himself its protector, and how you might be able to use these facts to your advantage, should you happen to, I don't know, travel back in time to find yourself face to face with a president you angered some-how. I'll never be president, but I can certainly beat James Buchanan in a fight, and, in the end, isn't that what American Government is *really* all about?

(I'm genuinely asking. I didn't exactly ace that class.)

I've been studying presidents since I was eighteen years old. This study has impacted every aspect of my life, is entirely responsible for the book you hold in your hands, and it never would have happened if an angry old man hadn't told me once upon a time that I would never be president. So thank you, sir. You have been a profound in-fluence on my life, freshman-year American Government professor whose name escapes me at the moment. I'll never forget you.

★ ★ ★ ★ ★ ★

★ ★ ★ ★ ★ ★

GEORGE WASHINGTON

CANNOT TELL A LIE: YOU'RE
IN FOR A WORLD OF PAIN

★ ★ ★

There are two kinds of people in this world: people who don't actively enjoy being shot at, and George Washington. Most of you are probably in that first group, and that's why no one will ever write a book about how to fight you.

The idea that Washington liked being shot at isn't conjecture, mind you. No one is saying that Washington *"probably"* enjoyed being shot at, based on his willingness to return to battle in service of his country; he *admitted* to it. In a letter to his brother about his time on the battlefield, Washington said, "I heard the bullets whistle and, believe me, there is something charming to the sound of bullets," which, according to rumor, prompted King George III to remark that Washington's attitude would change if he'd heard a few more. "Oh, ho ho, perhaps you're right," Washington may have good-naturedly said with a chuckle, before he beat the shit out of King George's entire army and ran America for eight glorious and strong-jawed years.

But we know all that already. We all know how badass Washington was. We all know what a good and just president he was. We know him as the Soldier-Farmer, as a man of the people. We know all of this, because everyone talks about how bright, and strong, and fair President George Washington was. So I'm going to talk about how he was probably *magic*.

Let's start with how Washington knew America was going to war before America even had an *army*. Sure, the seeds of discontent had already been sown, but war was not a foregone conclusion to anyone but Washington even in 1775, when the Continental Congress met for the second time to discuss what to do about Great Britain's unfair taxation practices. War was an *option,* but not a certainty at that point, at least not in the eyes of the members of the Continental Congress. Many of the framers, like Benjamin Franklin, still had great fondness for their mother country, and were eager to find a solution that involved working peacefully with the homeland.

But not Washington. Whether he could see the future and knew war was coming or he simply *willed* the war into existence, Washington was ahead of the curve. On his way to the conference—before war had been declared (or even discussed), before he'd been given command of the Continental Army—he stopped off to buy some books about war strategy, tomahawks, and new holsters for his guns. If that didn't send a clear enough message, he showed up to the conference *already wearing his military uniform,* while the rest of the representatives were trying to delicately handle this whole "revolution thing" diplomatically. It was like everyone else at the conference was discussing whether or not they should build a bomb and Washington had already lit the fuse. It wasn't just about finding another chance to challenge a bunch of bullets to a game of chicken (though, true, Washington never missed an opportunity to do so); he knew war was inevitable and wanted to be dressed appropriately.

And of course, Washington was right. War was necessary. Even if it wasn't necessary before, it was necessary *because* he said it was, because, for reasons that will never be clear to historians (but will be to people who accept magic as a possibility), the universe bends to Washington's will.

Here's one of the most important things you need to know about Washington: he should not have been able to lead America to victory in the War for Independence. When it came time to choose someone to command the Continental Army, Washington was chosen for his *popularity,* not for his skills as a general. He was brave and a great soldier, but he'd never commanded anything larger than a regiment and, when he'd been handed an entire army of untrained, undisciplined troops, he started screwing up almost immediately. He lost more battles than he won, and the majority of those losses were a direct result of his own arrogance and overaggressiveness. Yes, Washington, the man we all like to remember as the quiet, dignified, reluctant soldier, was a short-tempered fighter who never turned down a battle. Why? The same reason any president does anything: *because he could.* One of the biggest myths about Washington is that he had wooden teeth. This myth, while a cute little bit of superfluous historical trivia, isn't technically true. In truth, it wasn't his teeth, it was his testicles, and they weren't wood, they were stone-cold steel.

Unlike most soldiers (and, indeed, most sane human beings), Washington didn't see a battle as a means to an end, or as an unfortunate but necessary part of achieving one's goals; he saw it as a chance to show his enemies how brave and strong he was. And, as commander, he felt that his army should function purely as an extension of himself. He'd treat every challenge from his opponents not like a necessary evil that needed to be stopped as quickly as possible, but like a dick-measuring contest, and the Continental Army was the big angry dick that Washington was always eager to pull out and wave around.

In a dick-measuring contest, sure, that's a terrific strategy, but it's not great in a tough war, especially when your opponent is stronger, larger, and more experienced, and this over-aggressive dick-waving strategy blew up in Washington's face over and over again. He sent his men into battle even when the odds were stacked against them, and he refused to retreat or back down even at the cost of human lives, all because he wanted his enemy to know that they weren't as brave as he was (read: their dicks weren't as big and crazy as his). At many times during the war, it seemed that America's favorite son was too arrogant and reckless to bring us to victory.

So how did it happen? How did an inexperienced commander with an unfocused and untrained army win the most important war in American history? The short answer, again, is "Probably magic." Washington firmly believed that Providence or fate was on his side, in everything he did. In the way that war was declared because Washington walked into a room and *said* war was declared, Washington won the war because he *said* he was going to. That's how Washington could look at loss after loss and say, "Huh, that's weird. I'm supposed to *win*. I guess no one told these guys I'm George Fucking Washington. No matter, I'll just go ahead and win it now." And he did.

Washington's tyranny of will didn't just determine the outcome of the war, it also saved his life. He would return from many battles unscathed but with bullet holes in his clothing, or without a horse (two different horses were shot out from under Washington—*in the*

same battle). This happened so many times that George Washington admitted on more than one occasion that he could not be killed in battle. He genuinely believed this, and the crazy part? *We have no way to prove him wrong.*

That's how a first-time commander won a war against the most powerful army and navy in the world: Sheer. Blind. Madness. Washington said he was going to win, and he did. He said he couldn't be killed, and he said it with such casual authority and certainty that Death was like, "Oh, okay. I thought I was supposed to end you, but you just seem so *sure.* You must be right. I'll . . . wait, I guess? I'll wait over here."

Even Death waited on Washington's orders before finally claiming his soul for that big battlefield in the sky. In December of 1799, Washington fell ill and a team of doctors tried for hours to restore his health. Having decided that he'd spent enough time kicking ass at being alive, Washington decided to try his hand at fighting ghosts, and he sent the doctors away, telling them to give up. The doctors could have kept him alive, but Washington had had enough. On his deathbed, Washington told his aide, Tobias Lear, "I am just going," and he died *while taking his own pulse.* You can almost see Death quietly sitting in Washington's room, waiting for permission to take his life.

So your best bet in your George Washington fight: Run. Run as fast as you can, though it probably won't do much. If Washington's already decided that he's won his fight with you, there's nothing you can do. George Washington, the quiet soldier who built our country out of blood and willpower, gives the universe its orders.

JOHN ADAMS:

THE CEREBRAL ASSASSIN

★ ★ ★

Let's get this right out of the way: Our first vice president and second president of the United States of America, John Adams, is much, much smarter than you. He's not the *toughest* guy in the world (we'll get to Teddy Roosevelt later), but he had one of the greatest minds of any president in history, and he regularly used that mind to accomplish seemingly unaccomplishable tasks. Like a great boxer who gets so tired of beating other boxers that he starts training and fighting armed grizzly bears, Adams dedicated his mind to fighting and winning the hardest and most uphill battles he could find.

In 1770, members of the British Army shot and killed five civilian men in what came to be known as the "Boston Massacre" (adjusted for inflation, five men from the 1700s would be about fifty thousand today, so the "massacre" bit actually holds up). The soldiers were destined to face trial, but no lawyer in Boston would represent them in court, because everyone knew that whoever defended the horrible British would: a) probably lose, and b) certainly be vilified by the rest of the British-hating Bostonians.

John Adams was not a man who cared about being vilified. Much like the thousands of reality television stars that would eventually fill the beautiful country he worked so hard to build, he didn't come here to make friends. He loved humanity, but didn't care for people and never quite figured out how to relate to and interact with them. He cared about his legacy and getting proper credit for his accomplishments, but he didn't care about fame or popularity; having principles and sticking to them was all that interested Adams. He had his ideals and his beliefs and his convictions and wasn't shy about sharing them. Being righteous wasn't just more important than being friendly or considerate; to Adams, it was *everything.*

That's why he took the *hell* out of the Boston Massacre case. There was no better way to represent his "Being righteous is more important than having friends" philosophy than by defending the British soldiers in the Boston Massacre trial. Remember, Boston in the 1700s was basically the *heart* of anti-British sentiment. People in Pennsylvania and New York, for example, weren't too angry with their across-the-pond oppressors, but discontent with Great Britain had reached a fever pitch in Boston, which is why the "massacre" happened in the first place. It would be convenient for us to believe that the British were needlessly cruel and evil, heartlessly firing shots at the poor, innocent Bostonians, but the less flattering truth is that the "innocent" civilians provoked the attack. They confronted the British in the form of a rowdy, unruly mob armed with clubs, and hurled garbage and insults in equal measure. Most *suggested* that the British start firing upon them. That's how much the people of Boston hated the British; they begged to be shot just so they'd have an excuse to demand independence. Many townsfolk later went to the post-massacre trial to intimidate the witnesses into testifying against the British. Now the soldiers were facing trial with a jury *full* of Bostonians and, if that wasn't enough, the witnesses were being tampered with.

John Adams won that case. That's how good he is. That's how *smart* he is. If Adams believes he's in the right, then absolutely *nothing* will stop him from accomplishing his goals. Boston was a ticking time-bomb of anti-British rhetoric, and Adams convinced an entire courtroom that the soldiers who shot and killed five civilians were in the *right*. (That's the equivalent to knocking out two grizzly bears with chainsaws, if anyone is still following the bear-fighting analogy.)

Adams continued his streak of fighting the hard battles years later at the Continental Congress, where he faced the uphill battle of convincing every other representative of the thirteen colonies that a revolution was necessary. Almost *everyone* wanted to negotiate with the British peacefully and avoid war at absolutely all costs. Only Adams and Washington knew for sure that a violent revolution was not only necessary but needed to happen *immediately.* Adams did it with his giant, terrifying brain. Richard Stockton, New Jersey's representative to the Congress, called Adams the "Atlas of American Independence" because of his dedication to carrying this cause on his back. You see, the Continental Congress was like a big street brawl, except instead of fighting with hands and feet, opposing sides traded long, passionate, and olde-tyme-profanity-laced monologues. You can call it "word-fighting" (or simply "talking," if you're a square), and Adams was the best word-fighter around. His speeches advocating independence were so heartfelt and convincing that he reduced grown men to tears. His most outspoken opponent in the Continental Congress, Pennsylvania's John Dickinson, was so devastated by John Adams's skill as a word-boxer that he resigned his position and joined the Pennsylvania militia. Dickinson was the guy who never wanted to resort to war—he wanted peace with Great Britain more than anything—but Adams's argument was so moving that he quit and picked up a gun.

Damn.

To put it simply, Adams just knew how to think and speak better than everyone. He knew how to get inside people's heads because he paid attention. Whenever he met someone new, he'd go home and write about them in his diary. How tall they were, what their hobbies were, what their strengths were, what their flaws were. Adams was an observer, and he used the information he gathered to cut to the core of people. He knew men well enough to know what they needed to hear to get them to see his point of view, and if they *refused* to join his side, he would take their biggest insecurity and shine the brightest spotlight on it for everyone to see. If you have shortcomings, he will find and exploit them.

You're at a disadvantage in your fight with Adams specifically because he's already the underdog. He was never a soldier (even though he would often tell his wife that he was jealous that Washington got to go out and fight battles while he had to dick around boring Philadelphia shaping the modern idea of Democracy), and physically, there's nothing too impressive about him. He smoked, he was overweight, he lost most of his teeth by the time he became president, and his hands shook. Despite all that, Adams lived to be over ninety years old, *in the 1800s,* back when people died at fifty and got married at twelve, probably.

That's exactly why you have to watch out for him, because unless you're *also* a toothless old guy with shaky hands, you've got the upper hand in this battle, and Adams *thrives* when someone else has the upper hand. He wasn't a man who often got in fights, so if he's fighting you, it means he thinks it's the right thing to do, which puts you in a very dangerous place. Remember, one of the other times someone went up against John Adams, Adams convinced him to quit his job and lead a militia to help defend *Adams's* ideals. *What do you think he's going to do to you?*

THOMAS JEFFERSON

JUST INVENTED SIX DIFFERENT

DEVICES THAT CAN KILL YOU

★ ★ ★

The worst crime I could commit as author of this book would be to let the brilliance of Jefferson's mind and the eloquence of his pen overshadow what a top-to-bottom, balls-out, unflinching badass he was.

Jefferson *was* a great thinker, and he *did* make a greater impact on American politics than any other person in history, but he was also supremely cool-as-shit, a fact that is rarely brought up in high school history classes. It's not *just* that Jefferson wrote the Declaration of Independence, the single most important American document ever printed (until now!), and it's not *just* that he personally invented more useful and persistent devices than any president before or since; Jefferson was one cold, above-the-law motherfucker with a taste for rebellion. (It says a lot about a president when the words used to describe him wouldn't feel out of place in the summary of a direct-to-DVD Steven Seagal movie.)

Jefferson may not have been skilled in actual combat, but that doesn't mean he didn't see the value in some violence every once in a while. When discussing war and freedom with William Stephens Smith, a U.S. representative from New York, Jefferson said, "The tree of liberty must be refreshed, from time to time, with the blood of patriots and tyrants. It is its natural manure." Basically, "Blood is the poop of freedom."

Jefferson truly believed that a country couldn't preserve its liberties if the government wasn't regularly warned that the people could rise up and take it down. He not only believed that the people should always be ready to question and threaten authority with violence, he encouraged it. *And he was the authority!* He basically took the office with his head tilted and his arms extended: the timeless physical representation of "Come at me, bro."

But Jefferson wasn't just about straight-up *begging* for a rebellion on his own soil (and encouraging future generations of informed Americans to take up arms whenever their freedoms get threatened), he also knew how to protect America abroad. For fifteen straight years, America was paying anywhere from $80,000 to $1 million every year to the Barbary States in exchange for protection from North African pirates. It was basically a mafia shakedown; if you wanted to trade anywhere in the Mediterranean, the Barbary States wanted you to pay "tribute," and as long as the checks cleared, the pirates wouldn't hassle your ships. For a while, everyone paid the pirates off.

All of that shit stopped on a dime (or nickel!) when Jefferson took office. Upon Jefferson's inauguration, the Barbary States demanded over $200,000 from the new administration, and Jefferson responded with the nineteenth-century version of "Go fuck yourself, pirates" (in sum: "Verily, good gentlemen of Barbary, go forth and fornicate upon thyself until the sun rises in the West and sets in the East"). The pirates responded with the nineteenth-century version of "No," which meant they declared war on America.

Now, at this time, it wasn't really clear *what* powers a president had when it came to war or defending the country. America was still new enough that we didn't yet have a system in place, and the Constitution wasn't super-clear, but that didn't stop Jefferson from sending out the newly formed American navy. Jefferson didn't *ask;* he told Congress, "I communicate [to you] all material information on this subject . . . I instruct[ed] the commanders of armed American vessels to seize all vessels and goods of [those asshole pirates]." Congress couldn't ask when Jefferson was going to send out the ships, because he already had and was only telling them as a courtesy. Congress was welcome to sit around and figure out exactly what he was allowed to do, and in the meantime he went ahead and sent out his navy to just wreck house on those pirates.

And wreck house they did. The war between America and the pirates—what became known as the "First Barbary War"—was quickly won by the United States and was the first time in history that the U.S. flag was raised on foreign land. It was also proof that America could command and win a war from home, and proof that the strength of the American military was not *just* reserved for the easy-to-fight-for cause of Independence. This was a military that knew how to fight *together,* under one flag. And who rallied those troops and made this war happen? Who started and ended a war in *just one presidential term?* Jefferson.

Still, don't let Jefferson's image as a badass overshadow the strength of his brilliant mind. He perfected designs for the plow, the macaroni machine, the polygraph, the dumbwaiter, and full-on invented the portable copy press, revolving chairs, and pedometers. We know he invented these things because he wrote about it in letters and his journal, but he never actually sought to get patents for any of them. This isn't included in this chapter to make you feel inferior (though, yes, you should), it's included because *someone* needs to give Jefferson credit for his inventions. Jefferson didn't think anyone should hold patents over inventions, so he never once filed for a patent, even though he was one invention-making son of a bitch. These are the actions of a man guided by principle, and a man guided by principle is incredibly dangerous in a fight. If Jefferson is committed to fighting you, not only does that mean that he's unflinchingly

convinced himself that your defeat at his hands is absolutely neces-sary, he's already invented at least a *few* ways to kick your ass (though his methods likely won't be patented, so feel free to steal some of those moves).

Of course, Jefferson wouldn't be a badass president if he didn't run his own life with the same iron fist he used to run America. Jeffer-son liked being in control, and his death was no exception. Jefferson had been sick for almost a full year before being committed to his deathbed. On July 3, 1826, he woke up and asked, "Is it the Fourth yet?" His doctor told him that it wasn't. Jefferson didn't say another word, but he peacefully held out for *seventeen more hours* specifically so he could die on the Fourth of July, for the fiftieth anniversary of the Declaration of Independence. Jefferson wanted a dramatic exit. He had a plan, and he wasn't going to let something as silly as old age, kidney failure, or pneumonia get in the way.

Even Thomas Jefferson's tombstone is impressive. It's fitting that he left detailed instructions regarding his tombstone. He designed his own marker and demanded that it read, "Here was buried Thomas Jefferson, Author of the Declaration of American Independence, of the Statute of Virginia for religious freedom, Father of the University of Virginia." Notice anything missing? At the time of his death, Jefferson was one of only *six people in history* to serve as president of the United States of America, but he was so casual about this fact that he explicitly told people not to include it on his tombstone, because it just wasn't a big deal to him. If "leaving your presidency off of your tombstone" isn't the nineteenth-century equivalent of "walking away from an explosion without turning around to look at it," then I don't know what is.

JAMES MADISON

WILL GO MEDIEVAL ON ANYTHING
BELOW YOUR BELLYBUTTON

★ ★ ★

In his lifetime, James Madison was called the "Father of the Constitution" by his peers, and while the importance of his role in shaping the laws that govern this country could not be overstated, they *really* should have called him Tiny Impossible Nightmare. But they didn't. Because none of the people who gave out nicknames in the 1700s were worth a damn.

Sure, Madison had one of the sharpest political minds America would ever have access to, but to understand how impressive Madison was, we need to spend some time talking about how terrible he was. Madison's life is one defined by being great at the things he was supposed to be bad at. He looked like anything *but* a president; he was 5'4" and only broke 100 lbs on his *best day* and before his midafternoon poop. His speaking voice was high and weak, so much so that reporters who came to see him speak often left blanks in their transcripts when they couldn't hear him, or simply gave up out of frustration. The man was a *president,* but his voice was so pansy-assed that reporters just couldn't be bothered.

It wasn't only that Madison's *voice* was awful; for a very long time, the things he used his voice to say were *also* terrible. Madison was part of a poetry/debate club in college and his work was *so bad* that he was the laughingstock of the nerd club. When he heard his work read out loud, he was so embarrassed that he vowed never to be a part of something like that again. Picture that. A 5'4", thin-voiced wuss who was the least cool member of his *college poetry club.* That is not the portrait of a future president. "A Poem Against the Tories," one of three Madison poems that have actually survived, concludes with Madison calling his debate opponents smelly. *That was his closer.* This is supposed to be one of the brightest thinkers in history and "You stink" is the most potent weapon in his insult arsenal? Come on, Madison, just because you're the size of a sixth grader doesn't mean you need to ape the trash-talk of one.

That said, calling his mean opponents smelly was maybe the only thing Madison did wrong while in college. When he wasn't wasting his time in strange, slam-poetry word-fight clubs, Madison was getting only four hours of sleep every night. Not because, like most college students, he wanted to party and eat too much; he simply wanted to get two years of work done in a single year so he could graduate earlier. And he did it. *While at Princeton.*

But he didn't major in fighting at Princeton, and you're getting a crash course right now, which means *Advantage: You.* Also, unless you're a child (don't be, there are bad words in this book), you're most likely fucking taller than Madison. Still, he may have been small, but he was *fierce,* like Napoleon, or a goblin. Despite or perhaps because of his height, Madison exercised regularly to make sure that his tiny frame could pack a punch. Unfortunately (for him, not you), he also suffered from epilepsy and arthritis, and there's no amount of exercising one can do to overcome that. One historian said he had the "frail and discernibly fragile appearance of a career librarian or a schoolmaster, forever lingering on the edge of some fatal ailment." Doesn't sound like much of a fighter.

Unless, that is, we're talking about *word*-fighting. Years after he'd graduated college, when Madison was called to debate political heavyweights like Patrick Henry (considered America's greatest orator) and James Monroe (another guy), he stepped up to the plate and debated the *shit* out of them. He debated Monroe, a much more experienced debater, outside in the middle of a snowstorm, got frostbite, and still won. It was quite an exciting moment in the history of the annual "We Should Have Just Postponed or Relocated" Debate Club.

Madison defied expectations. There was no reason this Chihuahua of a man should be able to best Patrick Henry in a debate, but he did it anyway, because hey, take a hike, logic, there's no place for you here in Madison's life. As long as poetry wasn't involved, Madison could convince anyone of anything. He was the one who shaped our Constitution, he was the one who wrote the Bill of Rights, and he was the one who wrote the majority of the *Federalist Papers,* successfully convincing the rest of America that the Constitution was worth ratifying. The tiny, whispery, least-cool member of the Nerd & Poetry Club was so bright and *so* persuasive that he eventually talked his way into the presidency.

You might know that Madison was a pacifist, and you might think that this fact will work to your advantage (or perhaps you only know that Madison was a pacifist because you just now read about it). Madison always believed that arguments should be settled with diplomacy instead of guns (though, sure, at 5'4" it's easy to be anti-war when you know that the average fourteen-year-old is bigger and stronger than you). But in 1812, as president, he felt that war was necessary. America's rights at sea were technically neutral, meaning the country was free to trade with whomever it wanted. Great Britain refused to respect this and tried to reduce the amount of trade between America and France, because Great Britain saw America as a threat to its maritime supremacy and because Great Britain is just such a baby sometimes. Madison tried reasoning with them, he tried to resolve things peacefully, and tried to politely ask the British to please just stop blowing up all of our ships, but they wouldn't budge. Even *Napoleon* thought it was a reasonable request (great tiny minds think alike), but Britain held out. So, having exhausted all of the peaceful options, President Madison declared war.

Two years later, that war came right to the White House. Even though he'd never fired a gun before, he picked up two borrowed pistols, hopped onto a horse, and rode out to the front lines. He had no previous military experience and was probably the most antiwar president we've ever had, but that didn't stop him from being the only man in history to take up arms and stand on the battlefield while being the president of the United States. Grant didn't do that. Teddy didn't do that. But President Mickey Mouse did, because Madison knew how to rise to a challenge (insomuch as standing on your tippy toes can be considered rising), even when all of the odds were against him.

This war, disparagingly called "Mr. Madison's War" by Madison's critics and the "Second War for Independence" by the people who actually fought it, was the end of America's economic dependence on Great Britain. (The first war, Madison maintained, was the "War of Revolution," while the War of 1812 was the "War for Independence.") Sure, this was the war that saw the burning of the White House, but it was also the war that gave us true independence *and* "The Star-Spangled Banner," and it was won on James Madison's watch. Tiny, fun-sized, peace-loving James Madison. He has overcome absolutely every single one of his many physical limitations and defied everyone's expectations time and time again, and his fight with you is just one more opportunity to surprise his doubters.

Still, just do that thing that bullies do when they put a stiff hand on a smaller nerd's forehead, taking advantage of their size and strength to keep the nerd outside of punching distance. Or, like, pick him up and throw him. This isn't a Bill of Rights–writing contest, it's a cage match. Grab that sucker, lift him up in the air, say "By the way, I'm a big fan of the Constitution, I'm really glad you put that thing together," and then shake him until his teeth fall out.

JAMES MONROE

WOULD LIKE TO WELCOME YOU
TO THE ERA OF NIGHTMARISH PAIN

★ ★ ★

It's unfortunate that James Monroe doesn't often get the kind of badass street cred that guys like Washington and Jackson get, because he kicked so much ass in the Revolutionary War that his foot has technically spent more time in an ass than it has in a shoe. Monroe was still in college at the start of the war, but that didn't stop him from rounding up twenty-four similarly angry patriots and breaking into the Governor's Palace (a place where the royal governors of Virginia lived and held parties). Weapons and ammunition supplies were short in Virginia, so Monroe took his men and raided the palace, stealing all of the decorative guns and swords and distributing them to the Williamsburg militia. Liberating two hundred guns and three hundred swords and driving the royal governor away for good wasn't enough for Monroe, so he dropped out of school and joined the fight. He never went back to school, which would have been a huge disappointment to his parents had he not chosen "the goddamn president" as his fallback career.

Monroe was an officer in the Battle of Trenton under Captain William Washington. Both men led their charge on the British camp and both men were shot. Washington went down (like most people) but Monroe just said, "Take as much time as you need, guy, I'll be captain now," and commanded his troops with a bullet in his shoulder. It was in this battle that Monroe managed to capture two *cannons,* because he'd gotten a taste of stealing guns from people back in college and took a real liking to it. In that famous painting of Washington crossing the Delaware, Monroe is the one waving the flag with the noble ferocity of a man who is clearly wondering if he can fit that whole flagpole up the ass of a British soldier.

Monroe took a few months off to recover from his bullet wound (the doctor at the time treated it by just sticking his finger in the hole for a while because *what the fuck,* right?), and went back to fighting as quickly as he could, getting promotion after promotion every step of the way. Monroe did so well in the military that he was eventually promoted to what would have amounted to a high-profile desk job position that saw very little action. Most soldiers *love* the part of the war where they're not getting shot at, but Monroe got restless, quit, and went back to Virginia to try to *start his own militia.* That's like if the star quarterback left the winning team in the fourth quarter of the Super Bowl, started a new team, and used it to *conquer the fucking British.* But Thomas Jefferson took Monroe on as a legal apprentice before his militia could really get going, so he left military service, beloved by his men and respected by George "The Only Washington That Really Counts" Washington.

Even though he never got a degree, Monroe served his country as ambadassador to France and governor of Virginia—and, bizarrely, as secretary of state and secretary of war at the exact same time. He was secretary of state under President Madison, who made him secretary of war when the War of 1812 broke out. Monroe resigned his old job, but no one took over so he just said, "Fuck it, I'll do both." He continued doing the duties of secretary of state while formulating offensive battle strategies as secretary of war until a peace treaty was signed, after which he resigned his war position and went back to having just one incredibly difficult job.

Monroe continued his streak of awesomeness into the presidency. For starters, he delivered a speech that was written by John Q. Adams that Monroe called the "Monroe Doctrine," because that's one of the things you get to do when you're president. The Monroe Doctrine basically said, "Dear Europe, stay the hell away from me and stop touching my stuff. If I see your faces around North or South America, I will come at you with everything I've got, God Bless America, these colors don't run, land of the free home of the brave go fuck yourself USA USA USA!" Monroe explained that any European presence on his soil would be viewed as an act of war, and at that point America had a pretty good track record for going to war with Great Britain, so Britain took Monroe's "Get off my lawn" speech to heart and stayed away.

Even though Adams wrote the speech, it was a perfect fit for Monroe, who refused to be pushed around or intimidated his entire life. At one point during his presidency, he had a dinner for visiting foreign diplomats. One of them somehow offended another, so they rushed off to another room to lift their swords and duel. Monroe—as president—grabbed his own sword and joined them. He took up arms and yelled at them until they worked out their differences and went home, because goddammit can't we have just *one dinner* where everyone isn't trying to kill everyone else?

A few months later, Monroe's secretary of the treasury, William Crawford, barged into Monroe's office and demanded high-ranking jobs for his buddies. President Monroe asked for time to think it over and Crawford got mad and said he refused to leave the office until Monroe agreed. Monroe decided instead to flip out, grab a set of fireplace tongs, and shout, "You will *now* leave the room or you will be thrust out." It's not clear what he would have *done* with those tongs, but the fact that he grabbed them must mean that he had *some* kind of plan, and this author is too terrified to even speculate.

Something with the guy's balls, maybe? That would've been the worst.

Great Britain's decision to get off America's back also gave Monroe an opportunity to help America grow. It can be said that lots of presidents gave America her metaphorical balls (Washington with

his confidence, Teddy with his toughness, Lyndon Johnson with his enormous set of genitalia), but only Monroe can boast giving America her *actual* dick, when he purchased Florida from Spain. Monroe thought, "Truly, America is a majestic and inspiring thing of beauty, and yet I cannot help but feel that a mighty, swinging dong would really bring the whole place together," and America's been proudly waving that thing at passersby ever since.

As you prepare for your fight with President Monroe, remember to work his left shoulder. That's where he was shot, and that bullet stayed there throughout Monroe's whole life (most modern doctors recommend taking bullets *out* of the body). Avoid his punches, which will likely be very painful (he was tall and rugged, and everyone who met him talked about his "great physical strength and endurance"). If the fight comes down to a battle of wits, you could probably outsmart him. Monroe was a good president, but he simply wasn't gifted with a brilliant mind, like Adams or Jefferson or you (hopefully). He was described by Aaron Burr as "incompetent . . . naturally dull and stupid . . . extremely illiterate . . . indecisive to a degree that would be incredible to one who did not know him . . . [and] far below mediocrity." It was said that because of Monroe's stupid brain, he couldn't "shine on a subject which is entirely new to him." Unfortunately for you, fighting *isn't* completely new to Monroe, but still, some quick outside-the-box thinking might be your best friend in this fight (maybe try to throw him off his game by yelling something wacky or kissing him, right before you start brawling. Just spitballing, here).

JOHN QUINCY ADAMS

IS THE UGLIEST PRESIDENT
EVER TO BEAT YOU TO DEATH

★ ★ ★

At the age of eight, John Quincy Adams was made the man of his house while his father, John Adams, was off doing important John Adams things for America. This would be a lot of terrifying responsibility at any time in American history, but it just so happens that, when Adams was eight years old, the *Revolutionary freaking War* was happening right outside his house. The house he had sworn to protect. He watched the battle of Bunker Hill from his front porch, according to his diary, worried that he might be "butchered in cold blood, or taken and carried . . . as hostages by any foraging or marauding detachment of British soldiers." I don't have the diary I kept at age eight, but I think the only things I worried about was whether or not they'd have corndogs in school the next day and if I had the wherewithal and clarity of purpose to collect all of the Pokémon. John Q, on the other hand, guarded his house, mother, and siblings during wartime.

This isn't to imply that eight-year-old John Quincy Adams could have beaten eight-year-old you in a fight, but to imply that eight-year-old John Quincy Adams could beat you *as an adult*.

This experience, coupled with the fact that his father was John "I'm the President So If You Grow Up to Be Anything Other Than the President Also It Will Be Viewed as a Tremendous Disappointment" Adams (they can't all be as catchy as "Old Hickory"), inspired in Quincy his intense drive, sense of duty, and unstoppable quest for perfection in the pursuit of serving his country and living up to his father's high expectations. He was the private secretary and interpreter for the American minister to Russia at fourteen, secretary at the Treaty of Paris at sixteen, has held more diplomatic posts than any other American politician, and is the only president who served in Congress *after* his presidency.

As he got older, Adams only got *tougher* (he exercised regularly, swimming the width of the Potomac at 5 a.m. every single day, even as a fifty-eight-year-old president), and *more intelligent* (his skills as a diplomat are legendary), and *more naked* (he exercised, swam, and took walks in the nude, and called the art of having sex outside "in the open air, with the thermometer at Zero" a distinctly "Yankee invention"). It's a wonder that he even found time to have freezing-cold outdoor sex in between all of his exercising and working, but TV wasn't invented yet and folks had to occupy their free time *somehow*. John Quincy chose to bone in the snow and tell people how American it was, apparently.

This makes him a very, very dangerous opponent in a fight. I mean, right? There's a fearlessness and confidence inherent to being "the most naked president" that seems like it would really make him a force to be reckoned with in a fistfight. Also he kept an alligator as a pet, right in the White House. That too feels like something that might come up in battle. Like if you were walking down the street and saw a naked guy with an alligator on a leash, you probably wouldn't want to fight him, because to hell with that. That guy is John Quincy Adams, and it's too late, because you're already fighting.

Driven by his father's accomplishments, John Quincy was never satisfied. At sixty-five, he wrote in his diary that his "whole life [had] been a succession of disappointments. I can scarcely recollect a single instance of success to anything that I ever undertook." *What about that time you were president?*, his diary would have asked, if diaries were capable of asking questions in the 1800s, but John Quincy wouldn't have listened no matter *what* his diary said, because his inability to live up to the ridiculous expectations he set for himself drove him to depression, self-loathing, and intense self-punishment. The exercises that he did every day (for anywhere between two and five hours) had nothing to do with staying in *shape;* he was torturing himself for not being perfect. If he wasn't punishing himself with sprinting or swimming against the Potomac's current, he would soak for hours in ice-cold baths and rub his body down with a horsehair mitten, something that *sounds* adorable but is painful as all hell. John Quincy would engage in this intense level of self-punishment as *president.*

Even though he wrote most of the Monroe Doctrine and was instrumental in negotiating the treaty that ended the War of 1812, John Quincy Adams never believed that he was doing enough. If he brings that passion to his fight with you, you can assume that he's going to punch directly through you, then punch through whatever ground you were standing on, then punch any memories *of* you out of existence, and *then* punch himself a few times for not beating you quite hard enough.

It wasn't just his own body that John Quincy liked punishing; it was also his opponents. The only thing that gave him a more powerful emotional high than whipping himself with a cat o' nine tails was fighting his opponents, especially if he was standing alone fighting *multiple* opponents. His ego was fueled by victory and self-righteousness and, as time went on, he came to be feared in Congress for his ferocity, persistence, and habit of out-shouting the chair whenever the chair tried to tell him he was out of order (probably for shouting too loud). John Quincy spent every day believing that, in this life, it was just him against the world, and he *loved* this feeling.

He was also crazy, in case that wasn't clear from the ice baths and spike brush. Apparently, so much of his brain was devoted to diplomacy and naked fish races that there was no room left in that giant skull of his for the part of the brain that's supposed to focus on reason and rationality. While president (of, it should be stressed, the whole country), Adams was approached by a man named John Cleves Symmes Jr., who fervently believed that the Earth was hollow and full of tiny civilizations. He even drew a map of a hollow Earth with a bunch of busy little civilizations made up of mole people to drive his point home. *There are mole people living beneath us,* Symmes stressed.

Then John Quincy Adams, the Monroe Doctrine contributor

that we made president (once more, *of the whole freaking country*), *agreed with him*. He thought it was "visionary" and considered it his great fortune that *he personally* could help kick this expedition off and maybe open up trade relations *with the mole people*.

John Quincy Adams, a man smart enough to read and put on pants and make it through every single day without swallowing his own tongue, saw a stupid map about a hollow Earth full of mole people and thought, "Hey, I bet we can *trade* with those mole people! What do moles like? Sugar? Hats? You know what, it doesn't matter. Take a bunch of taxpayer money, go to the North Pole, and start digging." There's no exaggeration here. That was his actual plan.

Thankfully, Adams left office before he could actually see this plan through, and when Andrew Jackson stepped into the presidency, he shut the project down, because even he could see that the plan fell somewhere between Arguing with Cats and Eating Your Own Poop on the Spectrum of Stupid Ideas. The plan was too insane for *Andrew Fucking Jackson,* and he was so nuts that—Well, you'll see, I don't want to spoil it.

(He's really crazy, though.)

When he left office, Adams continued to serve his country in Congress. Fittingly, he fought and worked for his country right up until he was hit with a massive cerebral hemorrhage literally in the middle of answering a question in the House of Representatives. He was about to answer a question from the Speaker of the House when his brain, disappointed that all of the *other* brains get time off occasionally, just gave up and said, "Nope. We're done here."

Let's hope, for your sake, that his brain is feeling similarly lazy during his fight with you.

ANDREW "OLD HICKORY" JACKSON

IS A WAR HERO WHO WILL
"OLD KICKORY" YOUR ASS

★ ★ ★

ndrew Jackson, the wild-eyed, hard-fighting, hard-partying, cane-wielding, and ball-stomping son of a bitch who ran our country for eight years was a whole lot of things, and all of them were crazy. He wasn't always a lunatic, of course, he *aged* into it, like a fine wine, fermented with poison and stirred with an ax. If "violence and hatred" were a drink, it would never leave Jackson's flask, but it's *not* a drink, so instead he drank whiskey to fuel his rage. Jackson would hate with a "grand passion" and would "resort to petty and vindictive acts to nurture his hatred and keep it bright and strong and ferocious," much like the man himself. It's not said but widely believed that we had no use for the word "badass" until the minute Jackson was born.

Jackson's measured and practiced hate-lust started when he was very young. Jackson was born without a father and his mother died when he was fourteen. As a result, he anticipated death around every corner and was prepared to fight at any moment, which he did, all throughout school. Often picked on by very misguided bullies, it wasn't uncommon for Andrew Jackson to come home with bruises, scars, and scrapes. At thirteen years old, having bested every available schoolyard bully in a three-state radius, Jackson decided to fight the British in the Revolutionary War. At the age when most of us were gleefully discovering our genitals for the first time, Jackson was tackling fully grown British soldiers with equal gusto.

In 1780, the thirteen-year-old Jackson was captured by British soldiers and taken as a prisoner of war, along with his brother. He was ordered to shine the shoes of his captors and, like the tiniest badass ever, refused, which earned him a long gash down his cheek from the sword of his oppressor. He was then forced to march shoeless, wound-undressed, without food or water, and full of bright and shiny hatred for forty miles from one prison camp to another, all while suffering from smallpox. The smallpox killed his brother but was just terrified enough of Jackson to back off quietly. He lost his brother, beat smallpox, fought in a war, marched miles barefoot, and got stabbed in the *fucking face,* and that's just adolescence.

Having learned nothing about the evils of war, and because he simply had additional testicles instead of the part of the brain that regulates fear, Jackson went on to fight in the War of 1812 and the First Seminole War and, when he ran out of wars, he just went duel crazy. Jackson's been in thirteen duels *that we know of.* While some historians dispute this number, everyone agrees that he loved him a duel. Every other day, Jackson was out dueling. Dueling this, dueling that. He was one dueling motherfucker.

One duel in particular stands out among all the rest. In 1806, Andrew Jackson engaged Charles Dickinson in a duel over gambling debts. Though Dickinson was widely known as a good shot, Jackson allowed him to fire first. It would be irresponsible of me not to repeat that: in a duel with pistols, Jackson *politely volunteered to be shot first.* Dickinson fired, nailed Jackson almost in the heart, and started to reload. Before he could finish, Jackson shot him dead. The man plays "Punch for Punch" with *bullets.*

Were Jackson to challenge you to a fight, it would most likely be a duel with pistols at either dawn or whenever-the-fuck-Andrew-Jackson-wants o'clock. The man *lived* to duel, and you know there's only one way you can participate in multiple duels: you're really, *really* good at them. Losing a duel isn't like losing at soccer (unless your soccer league is really hardcore); you get shot and then you die. Between his dueling and his military career, Jackson had been shot so many times that scholars say he *"rattled like a bag of marbles"* when he walked, as a result of all of the never-removed bullets taking up residence in his body. The pieces of shrapnel that he carries around like internal medals of honor are about ten times larger than your balls and infinity times as armored.

Of course, there is a possibility that he'll choose to fight you with his trademark hickory cane, in which case you will also lose. In 1835, a lunatic named Richard Lawrence made the first documented assassination attempt on a president's life when he pulled a gun on Andrew Jackson. The gun misfired, so he pulled out a second gun, *which also misfired.* Later, upon inspection, both guns fired without error. Some historians blame the weather for the temporary misfiring, but it's pretty clear that the bullets, having previously consulted the *other* bullets rattling around Jackson's body, had no interest in getting involved with what would end up being a futile suicide mission, as every bullet knows that Jackson doesn't believe in getting shot to death. When Jackson was tired of watching Lawrence pull out gun after terrified gun, he beat the shit out of Lawrence with his cane until presidential aides had to restrain *Jackson.*

Jackson's not just badass by presidential standards. He's not just badass by *human* standards. He stacks up against John McClane and Shaft; the man is badass by *fictional hero standards.* He's badass enough to be entirely made up, except he's terrifyingly real and wants to kick your ass.

Here is what you need to know about Andrew Jackson: he is a man followed by tragedy. He lost friends, family members, and his beloved wife, Rachel. He never remarried after Rachel passed (shortly before he took office), and so America became his replacement family. And this was one family Andrew Jackson was determined not to lose. He loved, lived, and worshipped America; it completed him. Additionally, as the first popularly elected president, Jackson saw himself as both the physical embodiment of America and its sworn protector. If Jackson was one thing in his life, it was extra-strength, shit-hurlingly crazy. But if he was *two* things, it was crazy and loyal. An attack on Jackson meant an attack on America, and if he thought someone wanted to hurt America, you'd better believe he'd react like a crazed father protecting his children (assuming most fathers are nuts and, instead of fearing death like normal people, actively challenge it to fights).

Despite a legacy consisting of enough violence and death for twenty men, Jackson admitted to having two regrets on his deathbed:

"I didn't shoot Henry Clay and I didn't murder John C. Calhoun." In a life rich with murdering people for little-to-no reason, Jackson's only regret was that he didn't kill *quite enough people.* People like Calhoun, who, it should be noted, was Jackson's vice president.

No one is safe from Jackson's wrath.

MARTIN VAN BUREN

IS READY TO FOX YOU UP

★ ★ ★

Martin Van Buren was a shitty guy. Not just because he was a bad president (though, yes, he was), and not just because he was pro-slavery (though, for the record, it is the stance of this book that slavery was and is wrong). Van Buren was shitty in a very general sort of way, and with all that that implies. If you were related to him, you'd dread Thanksgiving every year because you'd know *he* would be there, with his stupid stories and overbearing shittiness. If you saw him walking toward you, you'd cross to the other side of the street, out of fear that his aggressive and practiced shittiness would rub off on you. If you two went to high school together, you wouldn't be friends with him. You'd be all "No, screw that guy, he's so very shitty."

It is my personal and admittedly ridiculous theory that Van Buren's schoolteachers are solely responsible for his shittiness. Looking at Van Buren's handwriting, and reading accounts about the man from people who knew him, all signs point to the fact that he was most likely born left-handed. His schoolmasters, worried, perhaps, that Van Buren was a witch, would regularly beat him in the hand with a cane until he learned to write with his right hand. This lesson possibly informed everything about Van Buren, because it forced him to act in a way that was counter to what was right. Writing with his left hand felt right, but he had been conditioned to do the *opposite* of right (which, yes, troublingly, in this case means using his right hand). As a result of this conditioning, from that moment on, Van Buren was determined to, at every pass, do what was wrong. Or, for the purposes of this chapter, what was *shitty.*

Early in his political career, Van Buren figured out how to exploit the game of politics. America was entering a political period wherein the people were really starting to shine, to step up and elect the candidates that *they* wanted, to show that power really *does* come from the people. Van Buren took a look at that promise and thought, "Oh, hey, I totally know how to cheat that." Known as the "Little Magician" or the "Red Fox" for his ability to manipulate and mastermind elections (like foxes?), Van Buren formed the Albany Regency in 1822. The Albany Regency was what was called a "political machine": a group of similarly shitty politicians who basically controlled all of New York government for over a decade. They didn't control the government by being *elected* into power by the *people* in 1822; they got together to rig New York elections and place their friends and relatives in important positions of power. And Van Buren was their leader.

Knowing that Van Buren understood how to game the political system as well as he did, it was no surprise that he would eventually become president. I should be clear, Martin Van Buren didn't want to be a *good* president, he just wanted to *be* president, and enjoy himself while doing it. He wanted the attention, he wanted the power, he wanted the status, and that was it. There was only one issue about which he was passionate, and that was his stance on slavery (pro!). In his inaugural address, Van Buren said, "I must go into the Presidential chair the inflexible and uncompromising opponent of every attempt on the part of Congress to abolish slavery in the District of Columbia," an appropriate prelude to the presidency of shittiness that would soon follow.

When not fighting Congress on slavery, Van Buren spent his time in the White House throwing fancy parties for his fancy friends and spending lots of money on furniture. As an ambassador to Great Britain (you know, that place America worked so hard to distance itself from), he fell in love with the parties and royal lifestyle (you know, that thing America worked so hard to make sure never corrupted its Democracy), and his autobiography is just page after page of name-dropping from this period. He wanted everyone to know how many famous royal people he met in England, and how many cool parties he'd been invited to.

Martin Van Buren loved the fanciness and respectability of British royalty so much that he tried to bring it back with him to America. He spent a fortune redecorating the White House ($27,000 of which came from the American taxpayer, which would be just shy of $540,000 in today's dollars) to make it a more appropriate home for the kind of aristocrat Van Buren wanted to be. Jackson was the people's president, a man who invited the entire nation to get drunk with him to celebrate his presidency. His successor, meanwhile, turned the White House into a palace, with policemen stationed outside to make sure no "improper" people ever entered. He dressed like a big, shitty Mr. Fancypants who thinks he's too good for us, too. Davy Crockett, a man composed entirely of iron and testosterone, described Van Buren as a "dandy" who would walk around "laced up in corsets, such as women . . . wear. It would be difficult to say, from his personal appearance, whether he was a man or woman."

Van Buren lived lavishly and was spending all of this money, by the way, during the Panic of 1837, the most devastating economic collapse in American history (until the Great Depression almost one hundred years later). Everyone was out of work and struggling and helpless and Van Buren was sipping wine, flaunting his resources, and enjoying the most relaxing presidency ever. His critics dubbed him "Martin Van Ruin," which I bring up only to let everyone reading

this know that I intend to use that as my own nickname, should I ever decide to enter professional wrestling.

Van Buren didn't care that everyone was trashing his name or that the country was falling apart on his watch, because he didn't have strong opinions. He avoided controversial subjects and, whenever he was asked his opinion on literally anything, he would dress up his answer in so much vague language and doubletalk that no one ever knew where he stood on any issue. While Van Buren was leading the Senate as vice president, Henry Clay tried to get a rise out of him by trashing his mentor, running mate, friend, and president, Andrew Jackson. Clay was determined to get an opinion—any opinion—from Van Buren, so he delivered a long, passionate speech condemning Jackson's entire administration. When the speech was over, Van Buren didn't agree with Clay but he didn't defend his president. He walked up to Henry Clay, asked if he could borrow his snuff (a tobacco for your nose), took two hits of it, and then *left*. Just walked out without turning back. It's like no one told him that coolly walking away is reserved only for people wearing sunglasses while an explosion happens in the background; *not* for people who just let their mentor get politically bitch-slapped in front of the entire Senate.

Van Buren, rightly and obviously, did not win a second term. He tried running twice more as a third-party candidate when his own Democratic Party refused to nominate him, but mostly he enjoyed his retirement in an alarmingly though completely characteristically shitty way. He sometimes gambled, but not at a casino or with friends, like a man; falling back on the lessons he picked up in his Albany Regency days, he would gamble on elections that he would personally rig. Rigging elections wasn't shitty enough for Van Buren; he needed to profit from them and dress it up as a fortuitous gambling win.

In your fight with Van Buren, I'd strongly recommend guarding your genitals, as he will likely fight dirty. That said, he never played sports, never hunted, never served in the military, and never did anything that didn't directly contribute to his fancy, party-throwing lifestyle, so you've likely got an advantage over him in the general fitness department.

Blacken his eyes, head-butt him, and sock him in the kidneys a few times—and look out for that left hook.

WILLIAM HENRY
HARRISON

IS GOING TO KICK YOUR ASS SO HARD

HE—OH, SHIT, HE'S ALREADY DEAD

★ ★ ★

William Henry Harrison was one of those rare men who had only two main jobs in his life: Soldier and President. A child of the Revolutionary War (when he was eight, Harrison's home was attacked by Hessian troops, which contrasts starkly with the cartoon watching that you likely did at that age), Harrison joined the army in 1791. Well, actually, he briefly studied medicine first but decided that taking life was much more exciting than saving it. And it all worked out because, as history shows, William Henry Harrison was *great* at taking life.

Harrison fought in the Indian Wars for a while, earning the admiration of presidents Madison, Jefferson, and Adams (and precisely no Native Americans), and toyed with leaving the military behind for politics, but even as a governor of the Indiana Territory, he was still fighting battles and leading attacks against the feared Shawnee leader Tecumseh and his Indian forces. In 1811, Tecumseh and his troops snuck up on Governor Harrison and his men near Tippecanoe, and even though it was early in the morning—and even though Tecumseh's men had the element of surprise on their side (Harrison's men were asleep when the Indians attacked)—Harrison woke up and, in two hours, drove the Native Americans away and burned their camp to the ground, effectively stopping any future Native American incursion into their territory. This earned Harrison the nickname "Tippecanoe," because, seriously, the guys who handed out nicknames did not have their shit together for a very long time. Tippecanoe led this charge and personally fought in hand-to-hand combat as *governor,* which, on paper, is supposed to be one of the least-fightingest jobs one could have (next to, perhaps, Professional Presidential Fight Historian). Harrison then quit being governor and rejoined the army for the War of 1812, because, even though he was fighting in more battles than any other governor, he *still* wasn't satisfied by the amount of fighting in his life.

Harrison was a man for whom fighting and battle was everything. He met his future wife, Anna Symmes, while on military business, and when her father (a prominent judge), disapproved of Anna's interest in him, Harrison dealt with the man the only way he knew how: as a soldier. When Symmes demanded to know how Harrison would support his daughter, Harrison immediately replied, "By my sword, Sir, and my good right arm." Some guys ask a father for permission to marry their daughters, and William Henry Harrison waves a sword around at judges. And it worked. Harrison won both Anna's hand *and* her father's approval.

After he had stabbed his way into a marriage, Harrison went right back to fighting the War of 1812, which involved taking back Indiana, Ohio, and Detroit from British and Indian forces and winning a decisive victory at the Battle of Thames (the battle in which Tecumseh was finally killed). He was a national hero, but he left the army over a disagreement with the secretary of war; Harrison wanted command of *all* of the armies, and the secretary thought it would be best to divide the army up and just give Harrison *some* of it. Harrison apparently had plans that he simply couldn't act on without

an entire army under his command, so he resigned. Congress would later investigate Harrison's resignation, conclude that he had been treated unfairly, and award him a gold medal. Once more: the man got a gold war medal for *quitting*.

Maybe it was because he still wanted to be in charge of the army without having to answer to any pesky secretary of war, but whatever the reason, as soon as Harrison retired from military service, he sought the presidency. William Henry Harrison wasn't like a lot of other war-heroes-turned-president. Most of those men (like Grant, or Taylor), just sort of stumbled into the presidency on the strength of their national popularity. Harrison *wanted* the presidency, and he was just sneaky enough that he didn't really care how he got it. In 1840, after trying and failing twice in his pursuit of the office, Harrison was prepared to lie.

The Whig Party wanted some way to distance their candidate, Harrison, from the incumbent Van Buren, so they turned Harrison

into a folksy, blue-collar hero, earning him the label of the "log cabin
and hard cider candidate." Harrison campaigned all over the country for years, reassuring everyone the whole time that he was a fun-
loving guy that you could sit down and have a beer with. But it wasn't
enough for Harrison to be *just* the cool, good ole boy; he also needed
to make shitty Van Buren look like an elitist aristocrat.

Harrison and his team started releasing flyers—illustrations of
Harrison next to a log cabin—to demonstrate his down-to-earth au-
thenticity and prove conclusively that he could be physically near a
log cabin (in a drawing, anyway). The Whigs threw parades full of
log cabin floats, folks drank whiskey out of log-cabin-shaped flasks
to show support (somehow), and America ate it up. In a time when
political machines were running things and it seemed like only an
elite few made it to Washington, it was nice to see Harrison, a down-
home, decent guy, seeking office.

Here's the thing: Harrison was about as down-home and folksy
as the cold and terrifying cyborg the Republicans ran in 2012. Harrison *didn't* live in a log cabin *or* drink hard cider. He had acres and
acres of land surrounding his mansion in Ohio, where he fought as a
prohibitionist to close alcohol distilleries. Van Buren might have been
shitty and elitist, but as a guy who was born and raised in a tavern,
he certainly had a better claim to the "log cabin and hard cider" label
than Harrison.

In the light of modern campaigning, where *every* candidate has
an image that's carefully constructed and maintained by a dedicated
PR team, this might not seem like a huge deal, but it was fairly revolutionary at the time. Harrison's entire campaign was based around
selling an image, not a person. Harrison didn't actually run on any
issues. His campaign manager said, "Let no committee, no conven-
tion, no town meeting extract from him a single word about what he
thinks now or what he will do hereafter." Harrison went along with
it, because he wanted the presidency. He wanted it bad enough that
he didn't care about his reputation, and he certainly wasn't above
rubbing dirt all over Van Buren's stupid name. Harrison's team even
started an ugly rumor that Van Buren installed a *bathtub* in the *White*

House (apparently in the 1840s only assholes bathed), and the public went apeshit. Can you believe that? A bathtub. Like a common whore!

The campaign worked (a lesson adopted by literally every campaign that followed). Seventy-eight percent of the voters chose Harrison, because they fell for the lie about how real he was. Harrison, the uncompromising war hero, let his ambition blind him to anything else and lied his way into the White House. Watch out for him.

Still, if you're looking for a good strategy for battling Harrison, you should maybe just wait it out: Be patient. This is a man who died thirty days into his presidency because he gave his inauguration speech outside during a freezing rainstorm without an overcoat or hat or gloves or anything else that might keep him warm. Maybe he was trying to show off how tough he was, or maybe he was still trying to play up his realness, because overcoats are for fancy people, and Harrison was a *man's* man. Or maybe he just thought, "Hey, I wonder what's the dumbest way I could die?" The point is, he delivered a two-hour speech in the cold, got sick, and died after being president for only a month. You should watch out for the good right arm that Harrison boasted about to his father-in-law but, if at all possible, just dance around, ride this one out, and before you know it, Harrison will completely exhaust himself to death.

JOHN TYLER

WANTS TO "ACCIDENTALLY"
PUT HIS FOOT UP YOUR ASS

★ ★ ★

John Tyler was born to be a rebel. No one knows what started it, but rejecting authority and taking matters into his own hands was simply in Tyler's blood. Some of us are Fonzies, and some of us are Ritchies, and Tyler was a Fonzie. In elementary school, Tyler disagreed with the headmaster of his school, which is standard, so he organized his fellow classmates and staged a *revolt,* which is *crazy.* Sure, we all *thought* about it, but Tyler did it, because he is a loose *cannon,* and while most kids grow out of their youthful rebellion phase, Tyler let it define him.

Tyler was always fighting with whoever the authority was, even if the authority was the president, and even if the president was Andrew Jackson. Tyler made a name for himself as a senator by repeatedly criticizing President Jackson, voting against almost everything Jackson proposed. Tyler did this despite the fact that Tyler and Jackson were members of the same party and, in fact, his vocal condemnations of Jackson were considered an "act of insurgency" by his party. Tyler was originally a Democrat like Jackson and stayed that way until, like a good little rebel, he got fed up with their establishment, quit, and joined a new party, the Whigs. He rose up the ranks of the Whigs quickly and was grateful when they made him William Henry Harrison's running mate. It's possible that Tyler would have fought Harrison, as he fought every authority figure in his life, but we'll never know for sure, as Harrison died before anyone had a chance to decide if he was a good president.

John Tyler was the first man to serve as president without being elected. He stepped in when Harrison died, setting a president precedent and earning himself the unfortunate but appropriate nickname "His Accidency." This was actually a fairly badass move; most people assumed a new election would be held, and some thought Tyler should just be an "acting president" until Congress decided what to do, but Tyler didn't give them the chance. Shortly after Harrison died, Tyler took the oath of office and flat-out *told* everyone, "Hey, I'm the president now. *Deal with it.*" He promptly proceeded to tell Harrison's cabinet that regardless of how they did things under Harrison, *Tyler* was in charge now. They were going to listen to him, and if anyone didn't like it they could leave, because *nobody* tells Tyler what to do. A pretty ballsy move for someone who had no clear or legal right to be so ballsy.

Tyler's first order of business as president was to piss off absolutely everyone. Whig leader Henry Clay expected Tyler to work closely with the Whigs (as Harrison would have done), but even *that* felt too much like manipulation to Tyler. Tyler vetoed most of Clay's proposed legislation, hurting the Whig agenda and also running counter to how the Whigs believed a president should behave (their idea of the presidency involved vetoing as a rarity, and Tyler was immediately pretty veto-crazy). One by one, everyone in Tyler's cabinet resigned out of protest, because he refused to listen to anyone who he thought was trying to influence or control him (which, according to Tyler, was everyone). When he didn't change his policy even after his entire cabinet resigned, the Whigs officially kicked him out of the party. This makes Tyler the only standing president who was dropped by his own party, and it's all because he was worried that the Whigs were going to try to push him around. John Quincy Adams tried to get him impeached, and his critics in the media dubbed him "The President Without a Party," setting a precedent for James Dean and any other future rebels who would go without things. Tyler's decision to alienate his own party (the first entry on a long list of colossal fuck-uppery) had a devastating impact on his presidential legacy. The Whigs voted against him at every turn, and, as a result, he accomplished very few of his goals and is considered "hapless and inept" by most historians. He managed to officially add both Florida and Texas as states to the Union, but because of his stead-fast refusal to play nice and make friends, he never had a chance of getting a second term and the American people saw him largely as a do-nothing president. With no party backing him for reelection, Tyler briefly considered forming his own party, but backed down at the last second because he was worried his running would split the vote between him and Democrat James Polk, ensuring an easy victory for Henry Clay, the Whig candidate. Tyler was always eager to stick it to The Man, and, as the guy with the most influence over the Whigs, Clay was The Man, so Tyler backed out of the race specifically to screw over Henry Clay, and it worked. It was an "If I'm going down, I'm taking you with me" sort of move, and it paid off.

In one final act of rebellion, Tyler spent his last few days in office throwing one amazing and legendary party. Tyler sent out two thousand invitations (though three thousand people eventually showed up, proving that even if the host is generally disliked, no one can turn down a free party), "eight dozen bottles of champagne were drunk with wine by the barrels," and property was destroyed.

Tyler threw this party for no reason other than to deliver a silly little pun. When Tyler left the White House shortly thereafter, he remarked, "They cannot say now that I am a *president without a party.*" Then he put on sunglasses and a wicked fucking guitar solo just *happened.*

After his presidency, Tyler retired to his plantation, which he

named "Sherwood Forest," as he saw himself as a Robin Hood figure, which is weird, because Robin Hood stole from the rich and gave
to the poor, and John Tyler stole the presidency and owned like forty
slaves, but whatever. Oh, right, the slavery thing, that's important.
Lest you think that Tyler's rebellious streak was all fun, you should
know that being a rebel *also* meant rebelling against the Union. Yes,
when Tyler left office, he joined the Confederacy and turned on the
nation over which he used to preside. He was considered a traitor,

and was the only former president whose death wasn't officially announced or memorialized by the White House.

It's difficult to tell exactly how Tyler would do in a fight. He was an excellent marksman as a hunter and formed a militia during the War of 1812, but his unit never saw any action. He wasn't exactly scrawny, but he wasn't built, either, and suffered from one of those diseases that a lot of people in the 1700s and 1800s had where you poop too much. You're at a severe disadvantage if you're coming from any place of authority, so do whatever you can to not look like The Man in your fight. Also, please win.

Beat this skinny punk for being a slave-owning traitor.

JAMES K. POLK

IS READY TO POLK YOUR EYES OUT

★ ★ ★

Who the hell is Polk?"

That's not *just* almost every average American's response to the question "What do you think of Polk?" It was also the campaign slogan of the Whig Party, Polk's opponents when he ran for president as a Democrat back in 1844. Polk's introverted behavior and lack of popularity made him the first ever dark-horse candidate. He received his presidential nomination solely on the strength of Andrew Jackson's endorsement (when Andrew Jackson tells his party to do something, *they do it*). Almost everyone at the time said he was a poor choice who had no chance of winning (the *New York Herald* said, "A more ridiculous, contemptible and forlorn candidate was never put forth by any party"), and almost everyone *since* has completely forgotten about him.

Which is a tragedy. Polk is one of the most underrated presidents ever, both in terms of his accomplishments and his position on the spectrum of badassedry. He was just a little guy, and was prone to illness as a child, but what Polk lacked in physical strength, he made up for in obsession with not being held back by his lack of physical strength. Biographer Charles Grier Sellers said that, as a result of his "early physical inferiority," he "drove himself ruthlessly, exploiting the abilities and energies he did possess to an extent that few men can equal."

The most important thing you need to know about Polk is that he was a man who accomplished what he set out to do, no matter what. He is literally the only president who knew exactly what he wanted to do when he got to office, exactly how he would do it, and exactly how long it would take. When he took office, Polk made a list of four very lofty goals that he was going to accomplish before his time was up (reestablish the Independent Treasury System, taking government money *away* from the banks and placing it in a special reserve that the banks couldn't touch; reduce tariffs; acquire some of the Oregon Country from Britain; and get California and New Mexico from Mexico), and he dedicated every second of his time to pursuing those goals. Polk's to-do list was impressive enough for most presidents, but Polk decided to do the political equivalent of tying one hand behind his back, saying, "Oh, and by the way, I'm going to do it all *in just one term*," and then he dramatically dropped his microphone and walked offstage (or would have, had microphones been invented yet. He probably just dropped a pen or fist-bumped his vice president or something instead).

Despite this ambitious plan, a combination of Polk's passion and intensity helped him pull it off. He accomplished all of his goals, including giving us Texas, Nevada, Utah, Arizona, New Mexico, Colorado, Wyoming, and Washington. He also got us California, first by trying to buy it, but when Mexico said "Uh, we're not actually selling," he just straight up took it from them in the Mexican-American War (a domestic war successfully taken care of in one term *and wasn't even on his list*). Polk made America bigger (which, as any scientist will tell you, means he also made it better), and he fulfilled America's Manifest Destiny by expanding our territory to the Western shores.

And he did it in less than four years, just like he said he would. When it was time to plan for his second term, Polk looked around at his accomplishments and simply said, "Nah, I'm good. Pretty much nailed it in one," and chose not to seek reelection. There's not a single other president in the history of America that can boast a similar success rate.

Not only did Polk knock his presidency out of the park in one term, he did it almost entirely by himself. Dubbed the "Lone Wolf President" by at least one guy who writes books about fighting presidents, Polk had a problem trusting anyone who wasn't his wife. Whenever he was faced with a problem, he opted to handle things himself, and that didn't change when he rose to the highest office in the land. He once said that he preferred to "supervise the whole operations of Government myself rather than entrust the public business to subordinates and this makes my duties very great." It was fortunate that the Democrats had both the House and the Senate during his administration, because Lord knows what would have happened if Congress tried to get in his way. Polk was simply a man who embraced the policy of doing something yourself if you wanted it done right. He had Congress to back him up, and, hey, it worked for him, and that's why today America is America "from sea to shining sea" and not America "from sea to wherever Mexico or Great Britain says 'stop.'"

He died three months after leaving office of "chronic diarrhea" and, let's face it, of "utter humiliation at dying from chronic diarrhea." He was fifty-three years old. It was a tragic end to an incredible presidency but also proof that Polk knew what he was doing when he chose not to try for a second term. He was put on this Earth to spread America to the West Coast and, having finished the work assigned to him, he knew it was time to go. He didn't just leave the White House after his work was done; he left *life*. The man knew how to quit when he was ahead.

Described even by his enemies as "the hardest-working man in Washington" (making him our James Browniest president), Polk's determination and passion drove everything in his life. Still, while Polk

can drive as ruthlessly as he wants, that doesn't change the fact that at the end of the day he's a small, sickly fellow without a tremendous amount of fighting experience. He had Andrew Jackson for a terrifying mentor, which is intimidating, but unlike Jackson, he actually *refused* to take part in duels when the challenge was thrown down, and never issued challenges even when his honor was insulted. There's more than a good chance that you've got Polk beat in terms of both size and experience, because he was so obsessed with politics that he never really got good at anything else, including fighting. He was terrible in social situations, he didn't have any friends, and he never bothered to have any children, because he didn't want anything to stall him on the road to political greatness.

If you're fighting Polk, then, your best-case scenario would be one in which your fight has nothing to do with politics whatsoever, because if that's the situation, then his heart just won't be in it. It won't exactly be a walk in the park, because Polk could seriously take punishment; at seventeen he underwent surgery to remove urinary stones, and this is the 1800s we're talking about, where "surgery" means "a doctor cuts you open and you're awake the whole time and your only anesthetic is brandy and *holy shit* modern seventeen-year-olds have it easy, comparatively." He can't throw a punch, but he sure can take one, so make sure you throw a whole lot.

Still, he was a great president and doesn't really get the credit he deserves, so when you're face-to-face with him in a fight to the death, maybe let him win? Just to be nice? Come on.

ZACHARY TAYLOR

IS READY TO PLAY ROUGH

★ ★ ★

It was said that Zachary Taylor didn't fear things he had not personally experienced, which, as a career soldier, proved to be a valuable asset; until such a time as death would prove to be worth fearing, Taylor would court instead of run from it.

Nicknamed "Old Rough and Ready" by his fellow soldiers, due to his alleged roughness and readiness, Taylor achieved fame and praise for his impressive military career. He first landed on America's radar in the War of 1812. In September of that year, Taylor was ordered to escort the eighty men, women, and children under his care (some soldiers, some settlers) from Fort Knox to Fort Harrison, where he would assume command. Unfortunately, the group was struck by malaria; twenty-four of Taylor's people died, and almost everyone else, including Taylor himself, was very ill. In an apparent cosmic test of one man's ability to handle one goddamn thing after a-goddamn-nother, just a day or so after Taylor and his people arrived at Fort Harrison, tired and sick and haggard, he got word that hostile Indian forces were planning an attack on the fort.

Of Taylor's remaining men, only about fifteen of them were able soldiers; the rest were either civilian settlers or soldiers who were too ill to fight. Without skipping a beat, Taylor recruited five random settlers and turned them into temporary soldiers. He gave all twenty of the men sixteen rounds each of firepower. On September 4, 1812, Taylor and his men were woken up at midnight when an invading horde of six hundred Indians set fire to their camp. The soldiers panicked (two of the experienced ones, in fact, fled the fort as soon as the flames started). Taylor was disoriented and outnumbered but apparently he must have accidentally left all of his fucks back at Fort Knox, because by the time the battle started, he had none left to give. So while almost anyone else in the world would have seen two choices (death by fire, death by Native Americans), Taylor, with a handful of troops and a bellyful of malaria, chose a third option: The Taylor Way.

After informing his men that "Taylor never surrenders," Old Rough and Ready calmly ordered some of his men to fix the fort's fire-damaged roof, and told the rest to attack the invaders. Taylor saw the flaming fort as a great opportunity, because the flames lit up the sky and revealed the attackers, and because he was crazy. A small chunk of Taylor's men put out the fire and worked to repair the roof while the *other* small chunk of his men held back the six hundred Indian attackers and provided cover. By morning the fire was gone, the damage was repaired, and the invaders had retreated. It was the first American military victory in the War of 1812, and Taylor pulled it off with a twenty-man army of soldiers and civilians.

Taylor's entire military career is full of similar stories. The Battle of Resaca de la Palma saw a victory under Taylor's command despite the fact that he had 1,700 men to Mexico's 4,000. He beat back General Santa Anna's army of 20,000 with just 4,500 men and what, at this point, we can only assume is a comical inability to understand how numbers and odds work.

Taylor was a great commander and soldier, if you asked his men (despite his high rank, he was always willing to march through swamps or woods or deserts alongside his troops, and pound on his enemies), but not if you asked his superiors. He had problems with authority that influenced every decision he made. Even in battle, Taylor refused to dress like a normal soldier and instead dressed like an angry old rancher, complete with a straw hat and duster. Every other soldier wore a sharp, well-kept standard uniform, but Taylor dressed like a gruff, furious soldier-cowboy because when he stumbled out of the womb, he was *already* grizzled and fed up with kids these days. Taylor was described as having a permanent scowl, half-closed eyes, wild hair, and coarse features—which, incidentally, is exactly how one could describe Clint Eastwood—which, double incidentally, is *awesome*.

Taylor's problem with authority earned him a lot of powerful enemies. When he was given direct orders (either in the War of 1812 or later in the Black Hawk War, or later at the Second Seminole War, or later at the Holy Shit Zachary Taylor Sure Fought in a Lot of Wars), he often treated them not as commands but as "suggestions," which he was always happy to "completely ignore." Taylor's gruff, no-nonsense, too-old-for-this-shit attitude, coupled with his reputation as a rebellious loose cannon, makes him, quite astoundingly, one of the only men in history who is at all times both Riggs *and* Murtaugh. He's his own buddy-cop movie.

After forty years of military service, Taylor retired from fighting and reluctantly accepted the Whig nomination for presidency. And I do mean "reluctantly"; Taylor once said that the idea of him being president would never "enter the head of any sane person." But we made him president anyway, because he was just so damn good at killing people (our requirements have since broadened). As president, he was hyper-aware of the fact that the slavery issue was very quickly going to drive the nation apart. He opposed extending slavery and publicly vowed to personally stomp anyone who disagreed. Literally. Half of the nation vehemently wanted to hold on to their slaves and revolt, and the president of the United States said that he would hang anyone who rebelled against America—and do so, according to his biographers, "with less reluctance than he had hanged deserters and spies in Mexico."

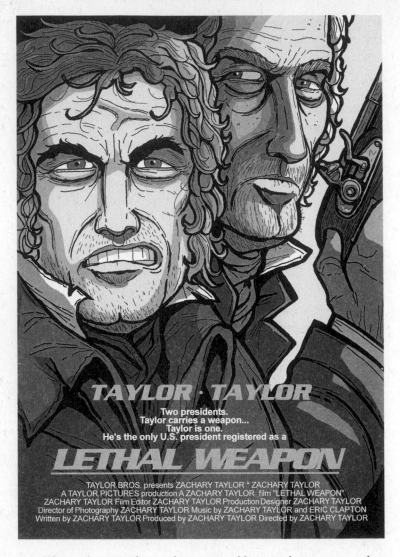

TAYLOR · TAYLOR

Two presidents.
Taylor carries a weapon...
Taylor is one.
He's the only U.S. president registered as a

LETHAL WEAPON

TAYLOR BROS. presents ZACHARY TAYLOR * ZACHARY TAYLOR
A TAYLOR PICTURES production A ZACHARY TAYLOR film "LETHAL WEAPON"
ZACHARY TAYLOR Film Editor ZACHARY TAYLOR Production Designer ZACHARY TAYLOR
Director of Photography ZACHARY TAYLOR Music by ZACHARY TAYLOR and ERIC CLAPTON
Written by ZACHARY TAYLOR Produced by ZACHARY TAYLOR Directed by ZACHARY TAYLOR

I know he sounds tough, *unstoppable* even, but everyone has a weakness, and Taylor's is adorable. Taylor died sixteen months into his presidency, not because he had angered slaveholders in the South, and not because he had angered the Whig party bosses who nominated him (they were hoping to use him as a puppet, while Taylor maintained that they were free to look upon his mighty crotch and "puppet this," whenever they felt so inclined). No, Zachary Taylor died by eating too many cherries.

On July 4, 1850, Taylor was at a fund-raising event at the Washington Monument. It was a particularly hot day and, to beat the heat, Taylor decided to eat some cherries—but, like, a *lot* of cherries. *Too* many cherries. More cherries than a person is supposed to eat. Historians aren't sure exactly how many cherries he ate, but the very fact that historians are even disputing the exact number of cherries consumed should tell you that it's a pretty freaking serious amount. Taylor got hot and ate an impossible amount of cherries and then washed it town with *way* too much chilled milk.

We will never know why President Zachary Taylor did this. No one has ever prescribed cherries as a solution to overheating, and no one has ever prescribed eating every available cherry in a five-mile radius for fucking *anything*. But Taylor was heating up and sincerely believed that the cherries and milk combination would cool him down. Almost immediately after he ate his weight in tiny fruits, Taylor became sick with a mysterious digestive illness and died.

To this day, no one knows exactly what killed Taylor. His doctor diagnosed him with "cholera morbus," which is *barely* a diagnosis. Cholera morbus was a nineteenth-century catchall for a wide spectrum of stomach-related illnesses, including diarrhea and dysentery and, thanks to Taylor, whatever disease is birthed by the union of digestive fluids and a metric ton of cherries. It was basically his doctor's way of saying "His stomach's fucked up and I don't know why." In 1991, his body was exhumed and examined but all tests for poison came back negative; but anyone with a slightly functioning brain has concluded that it probably had something to do with the lifetime supply of cherries he shoved down his throat on a hot afternoon.

Get a fistful of cherries and shove them down Zachary Taylor's damn throat. That's your only chance. And remember, Taylor does better when he's outnumbered or outmatched, so try not to be a better fighter than him (though that's probably not much of a problem for you, Guy Who Is Reading a Book About Fighting Presidents).

MILLARD FILLMORE,

ONE OF OUR MOST MILLARD
FILLMORE-ESQUE PRESIDENTS

★ ★ ★

Millard Fillmore is, hands down, the most under-appreciated and ferociously badass president we have ever had. His parents, paranoid to an insane degree, wanted their son to be mentally and physically prepared should the British ever come back to attack America (an eventuality Fillmore's parents were *certain* would happen in their lifetime). While most parents sent their children to school, Fillmore's started training him for battle from a very early age. They didn't teach him *standard* warfare; Fillmore's father was well versed in the ancient and mystical art of the ninja, and decided to pass it on to his ambitious and powerful son.

That's right. Millard Fillmore was a trained ninja at *eight years old*.

His parents would often blindfold him and drop him off in the woods with no food or clothes and leave him alone to find his own way home, which Fillmore *always* did. Regardless of how unfamiliar and unfriendly the woods were, Fillmore would find his way out, usually within the first twenty-four hours.

Still, Fillmore wasn't *just* a ninja; he was also unbelievably brilliant. He built his first robot when he was just nineteen years old, and when the government offered a handsome sum for his design, he destroyed it and burned all of his research. The government wanted to turn his robot into a robotic soldier, and Fillmore refused to let his ideas be used for death and destruction. He was the first president in space and is largely credited with the discovery of penicillin. For his first campaign speech, Fillmore did backflips until his opponents *wept and surrendered*. He is (so far) the only American president who had a tattoo, and, if you're wondering, yes, it was a sick dragon that occupied his entire back. He could pee lightning. Only like six people in the world can do that, and Millard Fillmore was one of them.

★ ★ ★

Full disclosure: I may have played with the truth a little bit. Not *everything* I said above might be considered "accurate" in any sort of "factual" way, though I do maintain that it's all true in a broader albeit less truthful sort of way.

Okay, my publisher has informed me that I need to be more specific. The only true things about the above paragraphs are: 1) We had a president named Millard Fillmore, and 2) He had parents.

I'm sorry. I know this book is about pointing out interesting *true* facts about presidents, and for every other chapter, that's exactly what I did, but holy crap, Millard Fillmore is just *terrible.* If you've never locked yourself in your apartment with eleven books about our thirteenth president only to come away with absolutely nothing interesting or usable while a deadline looms over your head, then you'll never truly understand frustration. That's me. I did that. I read more about Millard Fillmore than any man should, and the only conclusion I've arrived at is that Millard "Not Even Cool Enough to Get a Nickname" Fillmore sucks and is boring and sucks.

Plus, "Millard"? Come on; get a real name, you jerk.

Few men can start with nothing, pick themselves up by their bootstraps, and proclaim proudly, "Someday, I'm going to be president on the off chance that the *real* president dies suddenly and I happen to be vice president at that time."

Millard Fillmore is such a man.

It's crazy, because his life story so closely mirrors Lincoln's (both were born poor in log cabins, both were mostly self-taught, both were members of the Whig Party early on, both studied law, both eventually became president), except Fillmore didn't do *any* of the cool or noble things that Lincoln did. He even publicly opposed Lincoln on slavery, because that's high up on the list of things that assholes are supposed to do.

No one wanted him to be president. He was only named vice president in the first place because he lived in New York, and the Whig Party wanted a Northeastern fancy boy to balance out Taylor, a rough Southern cowboy who was considered off-putting by Northern Whigs. That's it. The Whigs needed someone to balance their ticket who was the opposite of a cowboy war hero, and boy did they find him.

As soon as Taylor died and Fillmore took office, *the entire cabinet resigned* and his own party didn't support him for reelection. He was mostly responsible for getting the Compromise of 1850 passed, which eased tensions between the northern free states and southern slave states. (Temporarily, obviously. We still Civil Warred about it.) The Compromise, while good for America, was incredibly divisive for Fillmore's Whig Party. Some, like Lincoln, fled the party for the newly formed Republican Party, and some tried to form their own party while the Whig presence in the South just vanished completely. Whatever Whigs remained agreed on one thing: they did not want to endorse Fillmore as their nominee in the next election. Like Tyler before him, Fillmore was dropped by his party, but Fillmore's Compromise did more damage than the Whigs could handle. The weakened and scattered party ran one more candidate, Winfield Scott, in the next election, and when he lost in a landslide to Democrat Franklin Pierce, the Whig Party died.

No other president can say that they were singularly responsible for destroying a political party, so that's something. It's not interesting enough that I can write an entire chapter about it, so *go to hell, President Fillmore, you're no help at all*.

He helped open up trade with the Japanese, ending Japan's isolationism. Is that badass? No? Okay. During the Civil War he formed a militia out of men over forty-five, but the only "action" they saw involved marching in parades. Never mind.

Oh! There is one *kind* of cool story about Fillmore. After his presidency, he was offered an honorary Doctor of Civil Law by the University of Oxford, but he declined on the grounds that he had no formal or classical education, and therefore didn't deserve the honor.

The diploma was in Latin, and Fillmore maintained that "no man should accept a degree he cannot read." That's sort of respectable. But, before you go ahead and consider Fillmore a class act, please know that after his presidency he also formed the Know Nothing Party, a political party that was sort of okay but mostly racist, and that during his presidency he casually protected slavery. Because Fillmore wasn't just a boring and bad president, he was a dick, but also not an INTERESTING enough dick to make this or any other essay about Millard Fillmore halfway readable because *goddammit Millard Fillmore, you are the worst*.

His party believed him to be a traitor, as did the people in his home state of New York; he's consistently ranked as the fifth or sixth worst president of all time; he signed and obsessively supported the Fugitive Slave Act (the most oppressive law in American history); and now you're about to fight him. Please enjoy this fight. He's not too tough—he was a sturdily built guy who did his fair share of chores while growing up—but he also worked as a cloth-maker's apprentice, which doesn't do much in terms of toughening a man up. Poke him in the eyes. Slap him in his stupid face. Just standard fight stuff, really; you're going to win because Millard Fillmore sucks at everything except sucking, at which he stands alone as champion.

They say that thirteen is an unlucky number, so it's no surprise that our thirteenth president ended up on the wrong side of history and morality, and as fun as it might be to ramble on and on about the number thirteen and superstition and unfortunate legacies and *what it all means,* I'd be much happier watching you beat the crap out of a guy named Millard, so please do that.

Fuck Millard Fillmore.

FRANKLIN PIERCE

IS THE FRANKLIN PIERCE OF FIGHTING, WHICH IS TO SAY, HE IS A BAD FIGHTER

★ ★ ★

Widely regarded as one of the handsomest presidents, Franklin Pierce was your typical pretty boy, which gives credence to my longstanding theory that pretty boys can't really be president for shit. Your average American doesn't remember even having a president named Pierce, and even the most sympathetic biography ever written on the man admits that "not a single achievement can be credited to his administration."

Not that you should feel *bad* for Pierce. Pierce had a reputation for being incredibly likable his whole life, but behind closed doors, he was a stone-cold son of a bitch, a quality plenty of presidents share but one that Pierce *embodied*. His wife, Jane, a lovable and fiercely loyal spouse, asked him to make only one promise to her: he would stay out of politics. She saw ambition in her husband's eyes, but as much as she'd support him in almost anything, she *abhorred* politics, and with good reason. At this point in American history, it was already clear to many, including Jane, that the presidency was a killing job that took a toll on the president as well as his family. Jane needed only to hear stories of Andrew Jackson's wife dying from the grief and stress of being a presidential candidate's wife once to know that she didn't want any part of it. She didn't want to live in Washington and didn't want her husband consumed by the stress, depression, and overtime inherent to a career in politics. Pierce was already a popular player in the Democratic Party (in 1836, the youngest U.S. Representative at the time), but he left politics and opened up a law office to please his wife.

That was her only request of him. She didn't even lose her cool when he went to go fight in the Mexican War without telling her first (even though, holy *shit*, that's quite a whopper to keep from your wife).

In fairness to Pierce, he *really* wanted to go to war. His greatest frustration was that, by the time he had reached his post, the war was almost over (the "over" part is most soldiers' favorite part of war). The night before one of the last major battles, Pierce came under enemy fire, was thrown from his horse, and severely injured his knee. His commanding officer honorably discharged him, but Pierce said, "No." He refused to go home, refused to sit out another battle, and said, "This is the last great battle and I must lead the brigade." Say what you want about Pierce's do-nothing presidency, it takes a special kind of toughness to tell your boss, "Thanks but no thanks, I think I'd rather spend tomorrow afternoon getting shot at, if it's all the same to you."

Pierce, weakened but still determined to achieve some battlefield glory, fought in the Battle of Churubusco the next day and almost immediately injured the same knee, because obviously he did, because *of course* he did, because war is very dangerous. His men tried to take him off the field and he *again* refused, because Franklin Pierce invested all of his money in blind confidence and was still hoping it would pay sweeping dividends. Even though he couldn't move, Pierce stayed on the field of battle, barking out orders and firing wildly from his place on the ground. He survived this way, all through the battle, and his soldiers never forgot it. He's the American, nonfictional version of the Monty Python knight who continued to fight even after his arms and legs got cut off.

And even though Pierce joined the war without telling Jane, and even though he almost got himself killed, she *still* stood by his side, because all she wanted was for him to keep his promise and stay out of politics.

And for many years after the war, he did. He kept his promise and lived a quiet, private life with his loving wife. And then he became the president—which, yes, is literally the opposite of not being in politics.

Perhaps claiming that Pierce "lived a quiet, private life" a couple sentences ago wasn't entirely honest. Even though he wasn't publicly campaigning for office, Pierce stayed in touch with his political buddies in Washington the whole time and quietly, privately, made sure that they all knew that, should someone nominate him, he wouldn't turn down the offer.

It wasn't *just* that he was running a whispered shadow-campaign despite his promise to Jane, but that he was doing it all behind her back. Jane was the only person in America in 1852 who didn't know Pierce had his eyes on the presidency. The day she found out Pierce was considering stepping into politics was the day a fellow Democrat informed Pierce that he'd received the nomination. The couple was on vacation together and Jane was absolutely shocked and blindsided by the news. Pierce grinned.

Pierce's decision to sneakily become president against Jane's wishes and behind her back did irreparable damage to their marriage. Tragically, not too long before Pierce was about to move into the White House, the train that carried Franklin, Jane, and their young son went off the rails and crashed. Franklin and Jane survived with just a few scratches, but their son died. This, Jane believed, was punishment for Pierce seeking office when he shouldn't have.

From then on, Jane wore all black every day and stayed away from the White House as often as possible, abdicating her hosting responsibilities (First Ladies typically hosted lots of parties and

entertained guests). Pierce just kept on presidenting, because that was the kind of man he was. He wanted power and glory, and nothing, not a crushing knee injury and not the love of his life or the loss of his son, was going to get in his way.

Which was weird, because he was a really crappy president. Pierce was more focused on the *job* than he was on the *country.* He spent so much of his time playing the political game and ensuring his spot in the White House that he never looked around to notice that the issue of slavery was very quickly ripping the nation apart, and that the president was going to have to do something about it. We were on the verge of civil war, and Pierce's inaugural address went on and on about the great period of peace and prosperity taking place in America. He was a solid politician but, as the book *The American President* puts it, was "timid and unable to cope with a changing America."

Also, he was arrested as president for running over a woman with his horse—but was discharged due to a lack of sufficient evidence. This doesn't relate to any grand, meaningful truth about Pierce, and it doesn't tie into anything about his character or administration or anything, it's just crazy. A president got arrested. For a horse accident. That's nuts. Anyway.

Like Millard Fillmore before him, Pierce was not nominated by his party after his first term. The antislavery members of the Democratic Party turned on Pierce when he vocally supported slavery as president, a position he'd hidden from the antislavery Democrats during his initial nomination process. Also like Fillmore, he made no real impact on the presidency and is largely forgotten today. Unlike Fillmore, he (probably) ran over a lady with his horse and got arrested for it. Wacky.

Know that, when you fight him, he will most likely be drunk. Pierce's alcoholism plagued him his entire life and only worsened when he assumed the presidency. Jane's love and support kept him away from the bottle, but with her removed from the White House, there was nothing to stop him from turning to booze whenever he felt stressed or depressed or literally any other emotion. Pierce wasn't the sort of fun and lovable drunk glorified in *Animal House* or the Grant administration; he was a *drunk* drunk. The tragedy of losing his son, coupled with the anxieties of presiding over a nation divided, exacerbated his drinking, and "Franklin Pierce is a drunk" was whispered all throughout Washington; his political opponents took great joy in calling Pierce the "victor of many a hard-fought bottle." When he left the White House and someone asked him what his post-presidency plans were, Pierce replied, "The only thing left to do is get drunk," and that's exactly what he did until it destroyed his liver enough to kill him. In your fight, his drunkenness could work to his advantage (as he'll be less likely to feel any pain in his inebriated state), or disadvantage (as he will be sloppy and maybe even peeing himself).

Here's hoping you get the peeing-himself version of Pierce, but if he gets on a horse, you'd better watch the hell out. There's nothing more dangerous than drunk Pierce on a horse.

JAMES BUCHANAN'S
WHOLE STRATEGY REVOLVES
AROUND WAITING FOR YOU TO
SPLIT IN TWO AND FIGHT YOURSELF

★ ★ ★

James Buchanan has the build of a fighter but the spirit of a bed-wetter. It was under his watch that America split in two. Modern historians have voted his failure in the face of secession as the worst presidential mistake ever made. Not that he actively *forced* secession, but his do-nothing attitude and his inability to take a firm stance on national issues left the Southerners no other choice—and, incidentally, it is that same attitude that will help you in this fight.

Buchanan's worthless presidency is a real shame, not just because it damaged the country, but because Buchanan showed such early promise as a cool little badass. In college, he could often be found breaking university policy by smoking cigars and drinking to excess on campus in the middle of the day, getting into trouble (he was temporarily expelled), and pissing off his teachers, because even though he clearly wasn't studying or taking school seriously, he was still getting better grades than *almost everyone*. He did well enough in school that he earned a special academic honor but, because he was such a smart-ass, his professors got together and decided not to give it to him on graduation day. He was like Zack Morris in that one episode of *Saved by the Bell* where Zack got a 1500 on his SATs, if Zack Morris smoked cigars and then eventually indirectly caused the Civil War.

Buchanan cleaned up his rebellious streak after college and enjoyed a series of very successful careers before his presidency. He lived by his often-repeated personal slogan, "I acknowledge no master but the law," which with its similarity to "I am the law" makes James Buchanan our most Judge Dreddian president to date. He was known for his sharpness, his perceptiveness, and his near-superhuman hearing ability (he confessed that he could clearly hear what people were saying even if they were whispering in a neighboring room). I'm trying to link his freakish hearing ability to his presidency in some way, trying to find some kind of big, profound connection between his hearing and his policies, but I can't. One didn't impact the other at all. I only bring it up because I think it's neat.

Buchanan rode his "cool college kid" reputation all the way to the White House. He threw a *ton* of parties as president and even wrote the official presidential liquor supplier once to complain that the bottles of champagne and whiskey they were sending weren't large enough ("Pints," Buchanan wrote, "are very inconvenient in this house, as the article is not used in such small quantities"). While Pierce was the scary and dangerous "Lifetime Movie-of-the-Week Drunk" that made people feel uncomfortable, Buchanan was the fun-loving and incorrigible "Frat-Movie Drunk" that made people feel hilarious and sexy (and, eventually, disastrously hungover). Buchanan would drink two or three bottles of wine *in a single sitting* and then top it off with some whiskey while still maintaining his composure. Plenty of ambitious men came to the White House and tried to keep up with the president, and all of them failed. The White House would have been wise to install a room specifically reserved for drunken senators and world leaders to recover from the fool's errand of trying to keep up with President Drunkasaurus Rex. His nickname would have been "Buchanan the Booze Cannon" if anyone around him had ever been sober enough to think of it. People saw Buchanan drinking J&B Scotch Whisky so often that they assumed the *J* and *B* stood for "James Buchanan" and Buchanan saw no reason to correct them because he was more whiskey than man, so they were technically right. Again, in case there are children reading this (shit!), it would be irresponsible to claim that being able to outdrink all of Washington makes you cool.

But it does make you *kind* of cool. And anyway it was the only rad thing Buchanan had going for him as president.

There is a longstanding and fairly well-researched theory that assumes that James Buchanan, the only president who remained a bachelor his entire life, was gay. Because we don't and likely will never know for sure, I don't feel I have the historical authority to say conclusively whether he was or he wasn't (James Polk called him an "old maid" and Andrew Jackson's nickname for Buchanan was "Aunt Fancy," but that's hardly conclusive).

So I won't talk about rumors, but I *will* talk about what a crappy president he was, because that's *definitely* true (and a very fun thing to do). It's easy to say that the American Civil War was inevitable, and war didn't officially start until Lincoln's presidency, but *secession* started under Buchanan. When people talked of secession to Jackson, Jackson threatened to hang every last one of them. This is where Buchanan's "no master but the law" mantra hurts him, because when people talked of secession under Buchanan's watch, Buchanan, handcuffed by the law, did nothing to stop them. Buchanan's official stance on secession was that while it was unconstitutional for states to secede, it was *also* unconstitutional for him as president to stop them. If that sounds to you like Buchanan is trying to stop people from seceding by threatening them with a completely unenforceable law, then you're exactly right. It was a bullshit copout; Buchanan was basically saying, "Don't secede because it's against the law, even though I won't do anything if you break it, because doing something is also against the law. So, please?" South Carolina chose to secede almost immediately, because *of course they did*. They asked Buchanan to remove Northern troops from South Carolina's Fort Sumter, and he would have, had one of his cabinet members not pointed out, "Hey, Mr. President, I don't want to step on your toes or anything, but just so you know, acquiescing to the South at this point in history would be *an act of fucking treason, you idiot.*"

With America falling apart around him, Buchanan got frustrated and turned inward to his cabinet, fussing and nosily interfering with the personal lives of his staffers and their wives. The South was threatening secession and seizing forts, and Buchanan just wanted to gossip and drink and throw parties and dance until his term was up. He couldn't *wait* to leave the White House.

In a fight, Buchanan is still a wild card, because he's so *mysterious*. While he never married, he did have one early romance and even got engaged to a woman, Anne Coleman. Their engagement ended suddenly, and then his would-be fiancée left town and died mysteriously; her physician recorded her cause of death as hysteria—though, since there had never been a previous case of "death by hysteria" ever reported, he admitted in his report that he suspected her death to be a possible suicide, caused by a self-inflicted overdose of opiates. No one knows why they broke up and no one knows why or if she killed herself, or what role Buchanan played in either, but the situation was suspicious enough that Anne's father forbade Buchanan from attending her funeral.

Buchanan certainly didn't make anything clearer, though he always maintained that, one day, everything would be explained. In a letter to Coleman's father after her death, he cryptically said, "It is now no time for explanation, but the time will come when you discover that she, as well as I, have been much abused." Buchanan similarly stated that he wrote a letter and sealed it in an envelope that would explain the strange circumstances surrounding his broken engagement, Anne's death, and his subsequent ban from attending Anne's funeral, but that the letter containing these answers could not be opened until his death. Shortly before he passed away from respiratory failure in 1868, he changed his mind and instructed his niece to burn this and every other letter she could find. We'll never know what the letter said, why Buchanan's former fiancée killed herself, or what his big revelation would have been. The only informed conclusion to be drawn from that whole story is that Buchanan was weird, paranoid, and *mysterious as shit*. History remembers Buchanan as one of our worst presidents (and his critics at the time often called the Civil War "Buchanan's War"), but history should *also* remember Buchanan as a man who left bizarre chains of secret letters and could hear through walls. Because that's objectively way cooler.

Buchanan could have been a great president but, at the end of the day, he choked. He had a greater intellectual capacity than almost any of the presidents before or after him, he was charming and perceptive, but when the going got tough, he faltered. Use that in your fight. Even though he's a bigger guy, and even though he was in remarkably good health his entire life (except for his death, where his health was very bad indeed), he still can't handle pressure. Challenge him in front of a bunch of people and watch him crumble.

ABRAHAM LINCOLN

IS LIKE A SLAVE-FREEING

MR. FANTASTIC IN A SWEET BEARD

★ ★ ★

braham Lincoln, the sixteenth president of the United States, was a mutant.

    I'm not just saying he was tall (though, at 6'4", he is still our tallest and fourth-beardiest president). I'm saying that physically, he had a disease called Marfan syndrome. People who suffer from Marfan syndrome generally grow taller than your average person and have longer limbs that, typically, are fairly weak. Lincoln refused to accept the "weak" part of his condition and strengthened his arms through years of farmwork (he built his first log cabin when he was *goddamn seven*), because why even *have* bonus arms if you're not going to make them the strongest and most powerful arms you can? A life full of log-splitting made Lincoln so strong that, by the time he was twenty-two, his skills were already *legendary*. Dennis Hanks, one of the men who lived in Lincoln's town of New Salem, Illinois, said, "If you heard his fellin' trees in a clearin' you would say there was three men at work by the way the trees fell." But it wasn't three men. It was just one giant super-president. Lincoln's neighbors would see him down by the riverbank using his extra-strength magic arms to lift, according to some townspeople, "a box of stones weighing from one thousand to twelve hundred pounds."

I'm not saying that there's an age where someone *should* be strong enough to regularly carry around 1,200-pound boulders (that's far too much power for one man), but twenty-two still feels aggressively, dangerously young for that amount of strength. If you ever see a twenty-two-year-old carrying a boulder that weighs anything more than 1,000 pounds, you'd better make him president.

Having super-tough Stretch Armstrong arms wasn't Lincoln's only superpower. To be clear, I'm not counting his strengths as a communicator as a superpower; I'm saying that Lincoln might have been able to see the future. The year of his first presidential election, Lincoln dreamed he saw two reflections of his face in the mirror. One looked normal and the other was pale, and gaunt, and awful. He consulted with his wife, and they concluded that this meant that he would survive his first but not his second term. And if that wasn't ominous enough, one week before his assassination, he had a dream that involved waking up in the White House to the sound of crying. He traced the source of the crying to the East Wing, where a number of soldiers stood around a corpse covered with a sheet. He asked, "Who is dead in the White House?" and a soldier responded, "The president. He was killed by an assassin." If Mr. Fantastic and Professor X had a baby, there would be *tons* of questions, but also it would be Abraham Lincoln.

And now you have to fight him. With a lot of the presidents in this book, it's hard to tell *exactly* what they'd do in a fight, because many of them don't have long histories of hand-to-hand combat, so more often than not I'm using their physical stats, mental well-being, and military history (if applicable) to make my best attempt at an educated guess regarding their fighting style.

This is not the case with Abraham Lincoln.

When he moved to New Salem in his early twenties, Lincoln quickly made a name for himself by finding the toughest guy in town, Jack Armstrong, and challenging him to a fight immediately. Armstrong had Lincoln beat in terms of fight experience and name coolness, but Lincoln, of course, had him beat in two very important categories: 1) mutant powers, and 2) being Abraham Fucking Lincoln.

Using his massive arms, the ones that carried 1,200-pound boulders all over town, Lincoln grabbed Armstrong by the throat, lifted him off his feet, shook him like a child, and then tossed him when he surrendered. *Tossed him.*

Armstrong's friends jumped in to gang up on Lincoln, who just laughed and laughed. Well, he didn't *just* laugh. He laughed for a little bit, and then he beat the shit out of all of them. *All of them.* You see, Jack Armstrong and his friends actually *were* a gang, called the Clary's Grove Boys, and they terrorized the town of New Salem with intimidation and drunken aggression. No one seemed able to stand up to them, so they basically ran the whole place. Lincoln came in, saw this unruly gang of thugs terrorizing the town, and, inside of a week, beat the holy Christ out of every single one of them. He saw what they were doing and said, "Hey, I know I'm brand-new in town, but I'm going to keep shaking your toughest guys until you all go ahead and fear me. The time will come when I will need you to vote for me, so you'd better do it, because—" and then he threw Jack Armstrong into space in lieu of verbal explanation.

By the way, Lincoln made good on that promise I just made up, the one about how people had better vote for him or else. Years after his fight with Armstrong, in his very first campaign speech for public office in New Salem, Lincoln spotted an unruly member of the crowd, and instead of politely asking him to quiet down (like literally any other politician hoping to convince his constituents he was trustworthy and coolheaded), Lincoln left the stage, walked into the audience, and picked the man up and threw him twelve feet. And that man's name was Who Gives a Shit Did You See How Far Lincoln Threw That Asshole?!

Lincoln wasn't just a jerk-hurling president with monster arms (though that would be a perfectly adequate legacy, were it the case), he was also a ticking time bomb of ambition. Everyone loves to talk

about how Lincoln was born poor in a log cabin, but he *hated* that part of his life and wanted nothing more than to rise above it as quickly as possible. He wanted to be remembered, he wanted the respect of his fellow man, but, mostly, he wanted *power.* He was obsessed with power and ambition; that's why Lincoln took his first job in public office (a seat in the state legislature) when he was just twenty-five years old, despite not having a job, a house, any money, or more than one year of formal education. He ran for office with absolutely no prospects, believing perhaps that he would just eat power to stay alive.

Four days into Lincoln's first session in the legislature, he introduced his first bill. The next day he started writing bills for *other* legislators. Lincoln was a man who was writing laws despite never having taken a law class in his entire life. He also never lost his fury. While still a public servant he would verbally attack Democratic opponents, and when a critic spoke out about Lincoln's bills, he threatened to give his "proboscis a good wringing," which is the classiest way to say "I'm going to punch your face" on record.

Lincoln hated slavery on a deeply personal level and was frustrated that, unlike most things he hated, slavery wasn't the kind of thing he could simply lift up by the throat and shake until it was no longer a threat. Instead, he had to content himself with attacking slavery the legal and political way. He also saw slavery as an opportunity, as an issue on which he could make his name. He knew he wasn't going to be a war hero, and he knew he wasn't rich, so the only way for him to stand out was to take a bold, public stance on a divisive issue, and slavery was just the ticket. He passionately spoke out against slavery and rode the notoriety it gave him to a position as chairman of the state legislature and, when that wasn't enough, president of the United States and, when *that* wasn't enough, decided to become one of the *greatest* presidents of the United States. Currently, Lincoln spends all of his time alternately haunting our money and appreciating the many monuments we've made in his honor from whatever position of power he no doubt wields in heaven (Vice God?).

But before all that, Lincoln exercised more power as president than any man before or since. Four months into his first term, he increased the army by 22,000, the navy by 18,000, and demanded a draft calling for 40,000 more men. He suspended the writ of habeas corpus (a legal action that stops presidents from arresting whoever they want), and proceeded to arrest whoever he wanted (in Lincoln's case, that meant over 10,000 Southern sympathizers). He made the arrests public, a brilliant display of don't-fuck-with-me-ship. He delayed Congress for four months so no one could stop him, and when it was time for reelection, he made all federal employees give 3 percent of their paychecks to his campaign.

Presidents, especially modern presidents, have so many eyes on them, and so many people to answer to, and a Congress that is often stubborn and difficult to deal with. There are so many checks and balances in place that, today, it would be laughable to accuse a president of being a tyrant. While I'm not calling *Lincoln* a tyrant, I *am* saying that he did whatever the hell he wanted for over four years. You know, like a tyrant.

That's who you're dealing with. A superstrong giant who can see the future and does whatever he wants whenever he wants to do it. Watch out for this guy. If Lincoln thinks for even a second that you're standing in between him and power, he will not hesitate to wreck your proboscis. Just straight devastate it. Just wring the ever-loving fuck out of your worthless proboscis.

ANDREW JOHNSON:

PRESIDENT UNDERDOG

★ ★ ★

Andrew Johnson, our seventeenth president, just could not catch a break. Ever. If there was ever a president who could be called our Charlie Browniest, it would be Andrew Johnson. Sure, he was president, so clearly there are worse fates to have, but from the minute he was born until the minute he died, Andrew Johnson was an underdog who never belonged *anywhere*. Born poor and raised without a father, Johnson never attended school and was sold as an indentured servant to a tailor when he was just a boy. His poverty made him an outsider in his own town of Raleigh, North Carolina, and he had to put up with being called "poor white trash" throughout his entire childhood. He taught himself to read and write, worked hard, and was kind to the people he met, but he never really overcame his low background, not in the eyes of Raleigh anyway. Still, he wouldn't let his detractors get to him; he was just going to keep his head down, stay sharp, and work hard. "Honest conviction is my courage," Johnson used to say. "You're still a poor and stupid son of a bitch," his childhood peers would likely respond before pulling a football away from him right when he was about to kick it.

While he was an indentured servant, Johnson studied and read and learned all about being a tailor, but, seeing bigger plans for himself, he ran away at the age of fifteen (his "owner" placed an ad in the paper offering a ten-dollar reward to anyone who returned Andrew Johnson). Johnson struck out on his own and started his career in politics serving as a mayor, senator, and eventually the governor of Tennessee, but unfortunately for him, he didn't fit in there, either. As a Southerner who supported the Union during the Civil War, Johnson was hated by all of Tennessee, even though his position was "Hey, I like having slaves too, but wouldn't it be better if we weren't all killing each other?" It might seem strange that someone so disliked would even get elected as governor, but because this is Johnson we're talking about, you have to assume that even his governorship was fairly Charlie Browny. A Tennessee governor in the 1800s was mostly powerless, *especially* a Charlie Browny one like Johnson. The Whig Party, while clearly on the decline nationally, was still very much thriving in Tennessee. Johnson couldn't veto anything because the Tennessee legislature was still mostly controlled by Whigs, and he didn't even really have the power to make any political appointments or influence legislation. He used his position as governor to raise his own profile so he could hopefully one day occupy the higher offices he actually sought, while everyone around him refused to call him "Governor" without throwing up those douchey, sarcastic air quotes when they said it.

Johnson moved on to the U.S. Senate but, despite his best efforts, Tennessee seceded in 1860. Most Southern Union sympathizers fled when their states seceded, but Johnson stayed in town to serve as military governor, a position appointed him by President Lincoln, a man whose authority a Confederate state like Tennessee didn't even recognize. This meant that he had the very unenviable job of having to hold the state together and punish anyone who was anti-Union, which involved shutting down Confederate newspapers, firing anyone in his office that didn't support the president, and arresting pro-secession members of the clergy. Needless to say, this didn't exactly make him a hometown hero. He stayed in Nashville, which was constantly under attack by Confederate rebels attempting to seize control, but he never let them take over, at one point swearing to his panicked staff that "any one who talks of surrender I will shoot." By the end of the war, Johnson had restored civil government in Tennessee, but that didn't stop the people from hanging ANDREW JOHNSON: TRAITOR banners all over town. Believing that "Despised Military Governor" was at least sort of a step up from "Powerless, Pretend Governor," Johnson again kept his head down, worked hard, and continued to do what he thought was right.

Unfortunately, if you ask the average person what they think of when they think about Johnson, they'll talk either about his impeachment or his drunkenness. Johnson was a good man and a hard worker but developed a reputation for being a drunk. Why? Probably because he was drunk as hell when he delivered his inauguration speech as vice president. That's probably the reason. Lincoln, for his second term, chose the Democratic Johnson as his vice president as a display of strength and unity to the wounded nation. Then Johnson gave a long, repetitive, and ridiculous inauguration speech as a display of how much whiskey is too much whiskey.

Johnson's speech, described by the *New York Herald* as "remarkable for its incoherence," was all about the important lessons he learned growing up poor, and how great the country is, and how he loved America because of the *people,* man, and how "I swear it's not just because I'm drunk, but fuck it, we should all just start a band." Various staffers tried to shush or pull him offstage, but he wasn't having it, speaking ten minutes longer than he was scheduled to. A senator at the time, Zachariah Chandler, said, "The Vice President Elect was too drunk to perform his duties & disgraced himself & the Senate by making a drunken foolish speech. I was never so mortified in my life, had I been able to find a hole I would have dropped through it out of sight." Johnson wanted to make America feel beautiful that

day, and concluded his speech by saying, "I kiss this Book in the face of my nation of the United States," and then *drunkenly kissing the Bible on which he took his oath.*

Of course that's only half the story. The thing about history is that it's written by the winners (also by me!). Even though Johnson was completely shitfaced for his wild, rambling speech, it wasn't because he was an alcoholic by any means. Most people who knew Johnson knew him to have a drink or two once in a while, but that's about it. In this particular case, Johnson had been sick for several months with typhoid fever, and his doctor prescribed him a few shots of whiskey. (Medicine in the 1800s, man. What a fun time.) Obviously the combination of the whiskey and his illness produced that absurd speech and ill-advised Bible-frenching. The story could have ended there, but history is written by the winners, and all of the winners *hated* Andrew Johnson. His critics were loud and persistent, and that's how Andrew Johnson, a self-made man who picked himself up and worked hard his whole life, went down in history as the drunken vice president.

Even the fact that Johnson was made president when he was is completely unfair in some grand, cosmic sort of way. Being president is never easy, but Johnson had to step up and fill in for one of the greatest presidents we've ever had, during Reconstruction, one of the roughest periods in our history. If Johnson had followed, say, Fillmore or Pierce or one of those other assholes, history would likely remember him more fondly. Unfortunately, his opening act was Lincoln, and that's a performance *no one* can follow. It would be like following the Beatles, except the audience hates you, and instead of being as good as or better than the Beatles, your band is *Andrew Johnson*.

As president, Johnson was as disrespected as he was as governor, military governor, and human being, which is to say, very. His secretary of war, Edwin Stanton, vocally opposed Johnson's reconstruction efforts and actively undermined his president's decisions in the South (Johnson wanted civil authorities to have control over the South, Stanton wanted generals and other military leaders in control). Johnson, who was trying to both heal a wounded nation *and* live up to his predecessor's legacy, had enough to deal with already and didn't need some uppity war secretary second-guessing him at every pass, so he asked for Stanton's resignation. Then Stanton refused. Then Congress, who *also* didn't respect Johnson, passed the Reconstruction Act, which a) took away Johnson's control over the U.S. army in the South, and b) took away Johnson's ability to fire any cabinet members without the approval of the Senate. It was a move specifically designed to keep Stanton's position secured, and when Johnson tried to fire Stanton anyway (Johnson ignored the

Reconstruction Act because it seemed unconstitutional to him, and also because "Come on, just give me a goddamn break, guys"), he was impeached. He managed to keep his job by *one single vote,* but the writing on the wall was clear. The people never wanted or expected Johnson to be president, his Congress hated him, and even his own cabinet members ignored and disobeyed him. Johnson was, again, on his own. It probably goes without saying that the Johnson presidency was unspectacular, but what the hell, let's say it anyway. Johnson's presidency was unspectacular. Johnson purchased Alaska for America, which was great, but sort of paled in comparison to Lincoln's slave-freeing, war-ending one-two punch.

Johnson is the most underdoggiest underdog who has ever underdogged—which, in a fight, might hurt you. If Hollywood tells us anything, it's that the underdog always wins. No one expected Johnson to amount to much of anything, but he gave himself an education and rose to national prominence and eventually became *president.*

Still, if real life tells us anything, it's that the underdogs *don't* actually win. Smack this stumpy, Charlie Brown twerp around for a while and remind him why *he* doesn't get to write history.

★ ★ ★ ★ ★ ★

★ ★ ★ ★ ★ ★

ULYSSES S. GRANT

IS THE DRUNKEN, ANGRY JOHN McCLANE OF PRESIDENTS

★ ★ ★

Ulysses S. Grant was put on this Earth to do two things: kick ass and drink booze, and he will never run out of booze, so you can assume he'll be sink-pissingly drunk for his bout with you. Also, saying that he was put on this Earth only to do two things isn't an exaggeration; Grant was a failure at literally everything else he tried to do, including presidenting. He was never a great student, he was never an athlete, and didn't have many friends. He wasn't a terrific communicator, and as president didn't make enough of an impact to make a dent in any historical polls.

Grant wasn't even a solid military strategist, which is probably why he won so much. What Grant had, and what almost any great general needs, was a deep, natural, and impossible-to-quantify instinct for war. It is an unteachable skill that combines instinct with practicality and total ruthlessness, and Grant had it in spades. He never so much as picked up a book on strategy, and never made any decisions on the battlefield based on trying to be one step ahead of the other guy; he just operated with a sort of primitive war IQ. Grant was simply surviving by fighting every single day and every single night; he was a mad fighter full of piss and vinegar and mostly whiskey.

Oh, right, the drinking. Nothing could stop Grant from drinking, not an important battle, and not even the soldier that Grant personally hired to stop him from drinking too much. Let's take that again. Grant knew that he drank so much that he appointed *an armed soldier* specifically to make sure he didn't drink during the war, and he still drank, and he *might have been right for doing so*. The drinking lowered Grant's inhibitions and helped him keep his cool in any situation. Hell, even President Lincoln admitted that he wanted Grant in command of the army specifically *because* of his drinking. He was an alcoholic, but he was, according to Lincoln, exactly the kind of alcoholic that the Union needed. Lincoln's casual acceptance of Grant's drunkenness is the strongest 1800s version of the "he's a loose cannon but, dammit, he gets *results*" speech that we will ever hear.

His constant drunkenness combined with his terrifying innate battle prowess made him impossibly great as a soldier and later commander of the Union Army, and by "impossibly great" I do mean that he objectively should not have been as successful as he was. He was regularly going up against generals who had more experience and skill and sobriety, and, like Washington before him, would often return from battle unscathed despite having had his horse shot out from under him, or his sword shot right out of his hand. He won because he was lucky, full of liquid courage, and stubborn. Grant admitted on more than one occasion to having an inability to turn back in battle after choosing to advance, an aversion based entirely on his own superstitions. He thought it was bad luck to retreat, so he fought and he fought and he fought and he *fought*.

But all hope is not lost, because you are holding a book about president-fighting, which—unless a book called *This Book Is Made of a Poison to Which Ulysses S. Grant Is Allergic* exists that I somehow didn't hear about—makes mine the best book you could possibly have in this situation. Grant drank as much as he did because he was cripplingly insecure, specifically about being naked. All of his fellow soldiers would shower outside together in the morning, and Grant was the only one who refused to be seen naked by any of his men. He would bathe himself alone in his tent, and not a single other soldier (not even his aides and helpers) was allowed to see him, perhaps because he was worried they would laugh at or say disparaging things about his genitals. John Quincy Adams swam naked every single day and *loved talking about it,* while Grant, on the other hand, steadfastly kept his genitals from everyone but his wife.

Now, this isn't a book about presidential genitals (that will be my next book), so it's not my place to speculate on whether or not President Ulysses S. Grant had weird balls, but I would like to float that out as a possibility before we continue. Again, it would be historically irresponsible of me to state "Grant's balls were super-weird" as a fact, as I am not an expert on how weird Grant's balls may or may not have been, but in the interest of thoroughness, I *would* like to leave it out here as a potentiality. Grant might have had weird balls. You can choose to ignore or exploit this when you fight him in a few hours.

It wasn't just his comically misshapen balls that made Grant uncomfortable. For someone who made a career out of killing and helping other people kill, he was notoriously squeamish when it came to blood. He hated the sight and taste of it so much that, on the rare occasions when he did eat meat, he demanded that it be burned to a near crisp. In fact, if it hadn't been for his magnificent beard, you might even confuse Grant with a woman. In his youth, he was small, slender, and rosy-cheeked, with a face like a little girl's face. Some historians have described him as "feminine" and "soft," and his fellow officers' nickname for him up until the Mexican War was the "Little Beauty." His light, sing-songy voice often startled people, who assumed he'd have a more commanding voice, one more appropriate for a commander.

I don't know if you've settled on what kind of fight you and Grant will be having, but if you could avoid using animals at all costs, that would probably be wise. If you've already decided that this battle

will take place on horse- or sharkback, there's very little this book can do for you. If not, leave the animals out, because Grant had a real soft spot for them.

Grant was rejected by both of his parents and not liked by the other people in his age group (his nickname before the "Little Beauty" was "Useless"), so he turned to animals. He rode and loved horses and spent all of his time outside, bonding with and talking to animals, the only things that couldn't reject him or ask him why his balls were so weird. He loved animals *so* much that, when he caught a teamster whipping a horse in the face during the Wilderness campaign, he flew into a rage, used profanity (the only time in his life he did this), and tied the man to a tree and left him there for six hours. It was the angriest anyone had ever seen Grant, and this was a man who tried to kill other men *while drunk*. If you so much as step on a spider while going toe-to-toe with Grant, you'll unleash an inner Hulk that you don't want to mess with. You won't like Grant when he's Drunk Hulk.

So, in your fight with Grant, assume he's packed on a few extra beer muscles, the kind that dull pain and turn everyone into a good fighter. The smartest thing for you to do is draw blood (his or yours), as quickly as possible, just to get Grant good and queasy. The second-best thing you can do is get a big crowd to show up and, if you can manage, get that president naked. He will *hate* it.

Probably because his balls are so weird.

RUTHERFORD B. HAYES

IS BAD AT LOSING

★ ★ ★

utherford B. Hayes is one of the lesser-known presidents, but he's also the most likely to kick your ass as soon as you count him out. He's one of the last in a long run of truly badass presidents, old-school men who chomped cigars and fought in wars. Hayes served in over fifty engagements in the Civil War and was shot several times, but nothing seemed to slow him down.

In 1862, as lieutenant colonel, Hayes was severely injured in a battle. He was shot in the left arm, the bullet splintering one of his forearm bones and tearing a blood vessel. He lost a ton of blood, but instead of bleeding to death like a normal person or fear-pissing himself to death like, let's face it, *you*, he *"continued to give direction to his troops and succeeded in scattering the rebels."* He collapsed to the ground and, in between vomits, would call out orders and even yell at his men if they seemed to be behaving cowardly. He did this all from a very exposed position, bleeding on the ground with vomit chunks in his magnificent beard.

In another battle, Hayes had his horse shot out from under him and was launched several feet while a bullet grazed his skull, and most of his men assumed he was dead. Instead, he was knocked out, and as soon as he regained consciousness, he shook off the fall (and bullet wound to the head), found a new horse, and just started fighting again.

That battle was in 1864, by the way, two years *after* Hayes got his arm shot up and doctors almost amputated it. Most soldiers would have just left the army honorably after an injury like Hayes's, but he recovered quickly and got right back to kicking ass. Two years might seem like an impossibly short amount of time, but it was par for the course for Hayes. He was born a weak and sickly child, so sick that his mother was afraid to show him any love; she assumed she'd lose him, and she didn't want to get attached. As a result, Hayes (whose father died before he was born) drove himself to excellence. He wouldn't be held back by his sickness or by the fact that his father was dead and his mother resented him; he was going to be big and strong and *president*. He started a daily fitness regime, involving hunting and running, that lasted until the week he died; even as president, he would wake up with the roosters and start exercising. Historians have said that, as a child, he developed "an unusual strength and muscular coordination," and it was this unusual strength that helped him in battle and allowed him to survive despite being shot *five times* in the Civil War. Even though he was sick, Hayes was going to grow up to be superhumanly strong, and even though he was shot, he was still going to command his troops.

Hayes wasn't just supposed to lose battles and his life; he was also supposed to lose the presidential election, by just about any conceivable metric. 1876 saw the end of the Grant administration, and while Grant himself was an honest and decent (albeit weirdly testicled) man, his administration was one of the more devious in American history, loaded with patronage and corruption. This was a time when reform was important, so the Democrats nominated

Samuel Tilden, a successful reformer who fought corruption as the governor of New York. And the Republicans picked Rutherford Hayes, who wasn't so much a "successful reformer" as he was "some fucking guy."

If Hayes had any opinions, he kept them to himself. He was chosen not for his policies or his ability to speak or his track record, but because, up to that point, he hadn't stolen anything or pissed anyone off. Hayes's history of being a strong soldier was just a bonus; really it was the "not doing anything wrong" thing that made him attractive to his party. The Republicans just wanted someone who had never stolen (prompting Joseph Pulitzer to yell, "Good God! Has it come to this?"). Hayes had a clean record and was generously inoffensive. Generally inoffensive? What more can we ask for? Let's make him president.

When Election Day rolled around and the votes started coming in, it was clear to just about everybody that Tilden had won; Hayes lost the popular vote and even wrote a concession speech. America would never hear it. Once the Republicans realized there were four states left to count (and that Hayes could win if he carried those states), they sent people armed with hundreds of thousands of dollars (and weapons) to make sure everyone voted correctly (in this case, "correctly" means "Republican"). Republicans were calling on vote-counters in South Carolina, offering anywhere between $30,000 and $200,000 for a Republican victory. An entire box of votes favoring Tilden in Key West, Florida, was *straight-up thrown out.*

The threats and bribery and back-alley dealing went on for weeks, until a special committee was chosen to decide the election. The committee had eight Republicans and seven Democrats, so the Republicans won and ol' Rutherford "At Least I Never Stole Anything" Hayes stole the shit out of the presidency. (This earned him the nickname "Rutherfraud," which, admittedly, is a more succinct nickname.) Hayes ended up being a decent president, seeing America through the end of Reconstruction and making great strides for Civil Rights, but he didn't make any friends in office and didn't do anything as president that was either scandalous enough to give him

villain status or exciting and progressive enough to give him hero status in the history books. Tired of the life of a politician, he chose not to seek reelection.

It's fitting that Hayes's death was more badass than the *lives* of most people. He was still strong and physically active in retirement, but life caught up with him in 1893, when he was seventy-one. On January 14, Hayes suffered some minor heart issue while riding a train to Cleveland. According to his travel companion, he briefly complained of the pain, then shook it off and casually sipped brandy.

The "minor heart issue"? It was a heart attack; he just hadn't realized it. No one did, in fact; doctors didn't even find out until years later when they examined his body and medical history. He had a heart attack and self-prescribed brandy and only died at his home *three days later*, on January 17.

Hayes was a well-built and tough man, and beginning with the start of the Civil War, he never shaved, so he's certainly got you beat in terms of beardiness. Hayes was known to say that "fighting battles is like courting girls: those who make the most pretensions and bold-est moves usually win," so expect him to come swinging right out of the gate. Still, this was a man who, his whole life, *should* have lost, but didn't. He *should* have died as a sick, fatherless child. He *should* have died from his wounds in the Civil War. He *should* have lost the elec-tion, because he literally did lose the election. Yet still, Hayes came out on top.

Rutherford B. Hayes is *due* for a loss. He's had it too good for too long. The man doesn't know how to lose; *why don't you teach him?*

JAMES GARFIELD

IS AMBI-KICK-YOUR-ASS-STROUS

James Garfield's presidency was cut so short (he was assassinated just four months into his first term), that most historians don't even include Garfield when they're ranking the best and worst presidents; there's simply not enough information to figure out his legacy. Luckily for us, there's ample information about his tenure as a badass.

Garfield grew up poor and fatherless in Ohio, the last president born in a log cabin (unless they somehow swing back into vogue). His schoolmates relentlessly mocked him for his fatherless status, because children are literally the worst people in the world (Garfield claimed he was "made the ridicule and sport of boys that had fathers and enjoyed the luxuries of life"). The only thing he knew about his father was that he was an accomplished wrestler, so Garfield learned early on how to defend himself, earning the nickname the "Fighting Kid."

Garfield never grew out of fighting, either. Years later, when he ran into a guy who "refused to obey" him, Garfield reportedly "flogged him severely," and the guy attacked him with a plank of wood for what Garfield described as "a merry time." Garfield retaliated with glee, after which the guy "vamoosed." I keep calling his attacker a "guy," but that should probably be amended to "boy," because the person in question was one of Garfield's students when he briefly worked as a teacher. Just remember that, the next time you want to complain about school. If Garfield was your teacher, he would beat the shit out of you and laugh about it.

Laughing and punching jerks weren't the only things Garfield could multitask; he was our only ambidextrous president, and if you asked him a question, he could write the answer down in Greek with one hand and Latin with the other, simultaneously, all while kicking you, if need be. That multitasking extended to everything; before he met his wife, Garfield dated three women. Simultaneously.

As a workout, James A. Garfield would juggle Indian clubs. That sounds whimsical until you learn that Indian clubs are large, wooden, bowling-pin-shaped pieces of wood that weigh fifty pounds. Lifting weights wasn't enough; Garfield would only be satisfied if his workout included the constant threat of having fifty-pound hunks of wood crash down onto his head. His strength and experience served him well in the Civil War, where he was a major general (the youngest man ever to earn that title) and received praise from his superiors for his bravery.

Garfield wasn't *just* a fighter; he was also one of the smartest and most well-read presidents we've ever had. He loved to meet with writers, engineers, and intellectuals and just sit quietly and learn from them. A senator from Massachusetts who knew Garfield in his twenties believed he could easily be a great success in either science, math, English, public speaking, or the presidency. Most presidents follow a specific path; they start as either lawyer or war hero, move on to become a politician, and then become president. Garfield was both soldier *and* lawyer *and* politician *and* math and science whiz. This is mentioned only in case it's humbling for you to know exactly how many things at which Garfield is better than you.

Garfield made it to the presidency after serving nine straight terms in the House of Representatives. While his presidency was brief, he did manage to make a dent in the corrupt spoils system (whereby people got government jobs based on either paying for them or being friends with the "right guy"), which was still dominating politics. As soon as he was elected, he was hit by a storm of office seekers, corrupt jerks who wanted cushy government jobs and power. Garfield, perhaps remembering the bullies who tried to push him around when he was a kid, would not be moved, and pioneered the Pendleton Civil Service Reform Act, making it law that all government jobs be granted on the basis of merit and merit alone. This made Congress very angry, because they weren't used to dealing with a president who was quite this pushy. Garfield politely reminded them that he was the *goddamn president*, not them, and that they were totally welcome to suck it. Worried that any objection would prompt the president to sign a mandatory "sucking it" bill into law, Congress piped down.

There's no way to tell how much of an impact Garfield would have made on corruption, because his presidency was cut tragically

short when a writer-turned-preacher-turned-lawyer-turned-lunatic named Charles Guiteau shot him twice in a train station. Guiteau believed that he was personally responsible for Garfield's presidential victory. Guiteau had, after all, delivered a speech in Garfield's favor to anyone who would listen (which turned out to be not very many people at all). Never mind the fact that Guiteau had originally written the speech for Grant, and only changed it when Garfield won the Republican nomination. And never mind the fact that the only thing Guiteau "changed" about the speech was the title; originally titled "Grant vs. Hancock," because Guiteau initially assumed Grant would be running against Democrat Winfield Hancock, Guiteau cleverly changed it to "Garfield vs. Hancock," though he left the body of the speech untouched. The point is, Guiteau wrote a speech in support of someone, and that was reason enough to convince him that he was instrumental in Garfield's victory. Guiteau felt that, since he had gotten Garfield his job, it would only be fair of Garfield to return the favor and give Guiteau a job. Specifically, Guiteau thought he was entitled to an ambassadorship to France, and when the job didn't arrive at his doorstep he felt betrayed. Guiteau maintained that God spoke to him personally and ordered him to shoot Garfield, so Guiteau cornered Garfield when the president was about to board a train and gave him one last chance to appoint Guiteau ambassador to France. When Garfield refused to entertain the delusion, Guiteau shot him twice.

Amazingly, Garfield didn't die. He was taken to a hospital, with one bullet still lodged in his body that the doctors couldn't seem to find. In an effort to track the bullet down, doctors utilized a brand-new invention, the metal detector. The doctors would start cutting and digging whenever the device sensed metal. They did this several times, but still they couldn't find any trace of the bullet, even though they got the distinct impression that metal was present every single time. This was because the bed frame beneath Garfield was made of metal. None of the doctors decided to check that, though. There was no time; they had a president to recklessly carve up and poke and prod using their filthy fucking doctor fingers. One of the doctors accidentally punctured Garfield's liver, and another introduced streptococcus into his system, because for a long time "medicine" was just a bunch of guys fucking around. Garfield held out for eighty days before finally dying which, *holy shit.*

This will be a very difficult fight. It took two bullets, streptococcus, and a whole team of the dumbest fucking doctors in history eighty days to take out the Garfield. If you can handle yourself with any degree of grace, you just might be able to win this thing. Garfield was strong, but clumsy and accident-prone. He had a nasty habit of accidentally chopping himself with an ax while doing chores as a child (fuck!), and when he briefly worked aboard a ship, he fell overboard fourteen times in six weeks, a bold move for someone who can't even swim. Fight him around axes and water and hope his instincts as a clumsy little ass-hat kick in.

INTERLUDE:

ASSEMBLING YOUR
PRESIDENTIAL A-TEAM

★ ★ ★

I can't predict the future. So while I'm not saying that several years from now robots will rise up and attempt to overthrow humanity, and that it'll be up to you to travel through time and assemble a Presidential Attack Squad to defend America, I *am* saying we'd all feel really stupid if at least *one* of us wasn't prepared for such an event. If you're ever tasked with organizing the A-team of presidents, this chapter will probably be more helpful than any other chapter in any book, ever.

Whether you're forming an action squad to defend the planet or just putting together a group of presidents to pull off some kind of elaborate heist, every good team needs Brains, Brawn, a Loose Cannon, a Moral Compass, and a Roosevelt.

THE BRAINS

You need someone who can make a plan and think quickly on his feet just in case that plan falls apart (which, if you're planning an

Ocean's 11–style heist, it almost certainly will). **Abraham Lincoln** is such a man. If you're talking about a guy who won't crumble when the heat's on and everything's falling apart, you want the guy who kept a cool head when the country legitimately fell apart. Lincoln didn't even have any military background when he took office, but as soon as the Civil War broke out, he picked it up *real* quick. He met with generals, he read books on strategy, he talked with his troops and confidently mapped out the North's strategy for victory, and saw it through.

A good Brains guy sees everything several steps ahead of everyone else, which makes Lincoln, as a man who *saw the future and predicted his own death,* uniquely equipped for the job.

Alternate Choice: Theodore Roosevelt

THE BRAWN

Every team needs muscle. The A-team needed Mr. T, the Avengers needed the Hulk, and Alvin and the Chipmunks needed Mr. T, on that one episode where Mr. T was a guest star ("The C-Team"). For your Mr. T, you're going to want someone strong, tough, and crazy. Someone who doesn't need to be the smartest or the nicest, but someone who knows how to punch until there's nothing left to punch.

You need **Andrew Jackson**. There's not much to say about his toughness beyond what's already been said in his chapter, plus I'm worried that if I type his name one more time, he'll appear and then I'll have to fight him and, even though I wrote this book, I am *not* prepared for that.

Alternate Choice: Theodore Roosevelt

THE LOOSE CANNON

Look, there's no reason to sugarcoat this: every good attack squad needs someone who can do what others can't do, someone who isn't afraid to get his hands dirty. He operates in a moral gray area and might not always follow the law to the letter, but he gets shit *done*. For this position, I cannot give **James K. Polk** a higher recommendation. In the 1840s, the "shit that needed to be got done" was

American expansion; we needed to stretch out to the Pacific coast to fulfill our Manifest Destiny. Everyone knew this, but Polk was the one willing to make it happen. Polk addressed Congress and requested permission to declare war against Mexico, claiming that Mexican forces had entered American territory and "shed American blood on American soil." Congress, obviously, couldn't say no to that. War was declared, Polk sent out the troops, and before anyone had a chance to investigate, the war was over and California was ours.

Here's the thing: there's significant evidence that Mexican forces not only didn't draw first blood on American soil but that a) they didn't even invade American territory, and b) they didn't draw first blood *at all*. A full investigation into the matter never took place, as Polk had riled the American people into such a fury at that point that anyone who tried to challenge him would be deemed unpatriotic.

Did Polk lie our way into this war just to make America stronger and further his agenda? We'll never know, but probably. Polk is the kind of man who can make these sort of tough, potentially illegal decisions in the interest of serving the greater good. What he does might not be very nice, but he does it well, and you'll definitely want him on your side.

Alternate Choice: Theodore Roosevelt

THE MORAL COMPASS

Without a strong Moral Compass, your team could fall under the pressure of your Brawn and Loose Cannon. You need someone pure steering the ship, a leader that everyone can get behind. Without Captain America, the Avengers would be consumed by ego and pissing contests. Without Leonardo, the rest of the Ninja Turtles would succumb to a life of attitude and pizza-partying. Without Moe, the rest of the Stooges would be lost in a dark world of violence and drug addiction. Every group needs a guiding beacon to remind everyone that they're the *good guys*. The obvious choice for your team is **George Washington**, who is already basically Captain America to begin with. Washington is the only president that no other president has dared to criticize or find fault with; he's the only man who could rein in the egos and personalities of the rest of the members and keep them in check.

Alternate Choice: Theodore Roosevelt

THE ROOSEVELT

Without a good Roosevelt, your team might as well just stay home and count their panties, because they'd be as good as dead out in the field. For this position, I recommend **Theodore Roosevelt**.

Alternate Choice: Theodore Roosevelt

Look, I'm not budging on this. If there really *is* a robot uprising, you can bet your stupid ass that the robots built a robo–Theodore Roosevelt ("Theodore Robosevelt"), and if you don't have the real deal on your side, you won't stand a chance. Roosevelt embodies every other archetype on this list and you'd be stupid not to have him. I guess you could maybe swap him out for Franklin Roosevelt, who is at an advantage by already being part robot, but if TR's free, your choice should be pretty clear. All Teddy, all day.

C.H.E.S.TE

CHESTER A. ARTHUR:

PRESIDENT SUPERVILLAIN

★ ★ ★

very president that's been discussed so far, and (spoiler alert) every president that is going to be discussed, was a very specific kind of crazy, a craziness cocktail made up of ego, passion, and ambition. Despite the craziness, however, the men and other men who have served our country were good people or, failing that, doing what they thought was best. Some were misguided and some were corrupted by their friends, but they all genuinely seemed to at least *try* to help the country.

Only one president in this book was a supervillain. Ladies and gentlemen, meet Chester A. Arthur, the Lex Luthor of the American Presidency.

To understand what kind of man Arthur was, we need to understand what America was like in the 1860s. The presidency was an obvious and showy position of power; everyone saw the prestige inherent in it, and everyone knew how influential and important the president was. But some men, some dangerously ambitious men, saw a *similar* position in the 1800s, a position that also had a ton of power, but that received none of the scrutiny, none of the checks, none of the balances that presidents faced.

After the Civil War, the political conversation behind closed doors was less about the two established parties, and more about the "political machines" that ran these parties. These machines picked candidates, they financially backed candidates, and then they either bought or stole elections. They were the power *behind* the power, and New York had the biggest and most controversial machine of all.

The New York Custom House was where the government collected tariff revenues on the majority of goods imported into the United States, and it was run by just three officials. Each was powerful, but one of these officials, the Collector, was more powerful than the others. The Collector was paid more money than almost every other elected official (including the president of the United States). The Collector had the power to hire whomever he wanted. And not just a small team; the average Collector had power over one thousand jobs, and he had the ability to fire these people whenever he wanted, and there was absolutely nothing they could do about it. The Collector's employees were *dependent* on him, so they all jumped at the chance when he asked them for favors, almost always in the form of political contributions toward the campaign of whomever the New York Custom House decided to back in a given election. Because he had so much campaign money and a ton of potential campaign workers, presidential candidates were *also* fairly dependent on the Collector. There's a lot of power and money and prestige behind this position but very little accountability, and it always attracted the kind of people who wanted power more than anything else in life (historically, a cartoonishly evil sort of person).

People vote, but the Collector was one of the only people in history who could actually *make* someone president. So Chester A. Arthur wanted to be the Collector.

To secure that job, Arthur made sure he was always making the right friends, shaking the right hands, and doing errands for the right party bosses, many of which involved breaking the law. Arthur did it and he did it with a smile. Pick any random party boss from the mid to late 1800s who, thanks to the watchful eye of history, has been exposed as a corrupt tinkerer in the big political machine, and I guarantee you, you'll find a quote from that boss praising Chester A. Arthur.

Arthur was spending so much time away from his family in his pursuit of this job that his wife, fed up with the late nights and the time away from home, decided she was going to leave him in 1880. Before she got a chance to leave, she abruptly got sick and passed away. The historical records show that she got pneumonia and died, and that's probably what happened. I'm not officially saying that Chester A. Arthur, like some menacing Michael Corleone-esque, cold-blooded, power-hungry monster, killed his own wife when she interfered with his plans, but I *am* pretending he did for the sake of making this chapter more interesting.

(this probably didn't happen)

Eventually, after enough wheel-greasing, glad-handing, and deal-making, Arthur got his dream job. The Custom House was being investigated for corruption and accusations of patronage and general awfulness, so the party bosses who relied on it wanted to hire someone who would seem honest and trustworthy to an outside observer to help them weather this investigative storm. Arthur was the natural choice.

Arthur did a great job. He sat at the top of the New York Custom House as Collector, greasing the wheels of the political machine and fattening his own pockets with kickback after kickback, and dealing with the outside investigation the whole time. One investigation made it clear that Arthur had forced an import company to pay a $270,000 fine (even though they were only *legally* required to pay $7,000), but even as these and other scandals surfaced, Arthur was reappointed by then-president Grant, because even the *president* was mostly powerless against the machines.

Well, not *all* presidents. Once Grant was gone and Rutherford B. Hayes stepped in, he started shooting this Custom House–patronage–political machine bullshit right to hell. He personally fired Arthur, who retired in disgrace among scandal and corruption.

Oh, wait, no, he became president. Scratch that; he took a pay and power cut and *settled* for being president. First, he became the Republican nominee for vice president under James Garfield. No one would have thought that Arthur could have been a good VP (he was a shitty, proven scoundrel who according to at least one super-great book that you're reading right now totally killed his wife), but he still got the job, because his ambition, as it always had in the past, won out. It's important to note that he didn't want the vice presidency so he could do any real good; he wanted a position that commanded a great deal of respect but required very little work, and the vice presidency had that written all over it. John Adams, the first vice president in history, hated the job because it was a waste of time and carried no real responsibilities; no one *wants* that job, except Arthur, because of the *prestige*. So he, more than anyone else in history, *campaigned* to be VP. He again shook the right hands and smiled his big smile at the right people until he swooped in and took the nomination away from Garfield's first choice, a personal friend.

He did it in a single day. It all happened behind closed doors and with a lot of shady whispers and presumably slimy handshakes, so we'll never know exactly how Arthur, a proven con man, talked his way into the nomination; we just know that he did it in twenty-four hours.

Then Garfield died and Arthur—who, again, only became the vice president to cash a paycheck and get back the respect he'd lost in his disgraceful exit from his beloved Collector position—was suddenly the president.

Now here is the craziest part. As president, Chester A. Arthur was *actually pretty decent*. He immediately started reforming the corrupt political-machine system, the one that had made him so powerful in the first place, and launched a series of investigations and supported a bunch of laws that would ultimately render these machines powerless. He did a lot to fight corruption and did a ton for civil service reform. He's actually like a smarter Lex Luthor. Lex Luthor's flaw, and the flaw of almost every other supervillain, is that they crave power *too* much and don't know how to quit when they're ahead. If we made Luthor president, he'd just try to use that power to become president of the world and then universe and never stop until a Superman stood up and took him down. Arthur, on the other hand, realized he was ahead, so cashed in his chips and left the table. He covered his ass by defanging the corrupt people that could potentially manipulate him as president, and then he just walked away.

Even though his legacy as president is mostly positive, never forget just how manipulative and devious Chester A. Arthur can be when he wants something. If Andrew Jackson was crazy because he overdid the "passion" part of the passion-ego-ambition cocktail that all presidents drink, then Arthur is dangerous because he got drunk on ambition. He worked his way up in the political machine to get the position that carried the most power and pulled in the most money, and he used it for everything it was worth, down to the very last drop. When that no longer suited him, he set himself up in the vice presidency, because once he'd gotten a taste for privilege and respect, he wouldn't be satisfied with anything else. And then he became president, and as soon as he realized there was nothing else the political machine could do for him, he worked diligently to shut it *down*. He's cunning. He's wily. He's a super-smart supervillain whom I've (obviously) dubbed "The Collector," and you need to watch your back around him.

A childhood friend of the twenty-first president of the United States has a story about Arthur: "When Chester was a boy, you might see him . . . watching the boys building a mud dam across the rivulet in the roadway . . . Pretty soon, he would be ordering this one to bring stones, another sticks, and others sod and mud to finish the dam; and they would all do his bidding without question. But he took good care not to *get any of the dirt on his hands.*" This means there's a chance that he'll get a bunch of brutes to fight his battle *for* him, but it also means that his lack of dirt-touching experience will make him weak, and squeamish, so you'll have an advantage if you actually *do* get close enough to hit him. If you want an extra edge, maybe cover yourself in dirt before the match.

GROVER CLEVELAND

IS A SNEAKY BRICK WALL OF PAIN

★ ★ ★

Stephen Grover Cleveland, our twenty-second president, wanted the world to know that he was a good and honest man. He held himself to a very high moral standard, and he claimed to live by it from the minute he was born until the minute he died. Literally. His last words were "I have tried so hard to do right."

Cleveland was a stern, efficient, no-nonsense type who believed in hard work (according to his staff, it wouldn't be out of the ordinary to see Cleveland working until three or four in the morning, several nights in a row). Character was important to Cleveland, a man who once said, "If we expect to become great and good men and be respected and esteemed by our friends, we must improve our time when we are young." Was that from a campaign speech? Or in his inauguration? Nope. Cleveland said that when he was *nine years old*, and he never grew out of it. You know what *I* said at nine years old? *Neither do I, because it was probably bullshit.*

Cleveland's whole life is littered with stories of him going to great lengths to do what he thought was right, both personally and politically. While Cleveland was campaigning, a woman he'd been casually seeing before his marriage approached him with a son and claimed that it was his. Cleveland didn't know for sure that he was the father, but he still financially supported the child and checked up on him regularly, because he believed it to be the right thing to do. As sheriff of Erie County, New York, he strongly opposed the death penalty and fought to outlaw it. He was unsuccessful, unfortunately for Cleveland (plus all of those dudes who got the death penalty). When someone did receive the death penalty, he *personally* performed the execution, which was almost unheard of. Executioners existed—there was no reason for the sheriff to personally deal out the death sentence—but Cleveland believed that upholding laws, even laws he personally hated, was important, and he wasn't going to force someone *else* to do it. This is a man with clarity of purpose.

Grover Cleveland made a good sheriff and a great politician because, in a time when political machines were sneakily making deals and wielding too much behind-the-scenes power, Cleveland stood tall as incorruptible. He never allowed himself to be seduced by office-seekers and special interest groups. "Public office is a public trust," Cleveland said, and that trust was sacred to him. Cleveland's goodness was superhuman. Biographer Allan Nevins said that he "had no endowments that thousands of men do not have. He possessed honesty, courage, firmness, independence, and common sense. But he possessed them to a degree other men do not." Mark Twain said that Cleveland's character was on par with *Washington's,* and Mark Twain was a dick to *everybody.*

That makes it all the more surprising to learn that one of the most shocking displays of presidential deception took place on Grover Cleveland's watch.

During Cleveland's second term as president, a cancerous tumor was discovered in his mouth. This was right around the time that presidents were constantly being followed by the media (they followed Cleveland all the way to his honeymoon, much to his dismay).

Cleveland knew that he couldn't simply check into a hospital without the media taking notice, and he was worried about the news getting out. He worried about the impact it might have on the national economy (already on fairly unstable ground). He worried about what the rest of the world would think if they perceived America's president as weak or sick. (And presumably he also worried about just, like, general cancer stuff.)

So the man who built his career around the image of incorruptibility staged a secret medical procedure. It was like an *Ocean's 11* heist except instead of sending a ragtag team of specialists into a casino to steal a bunch of money, Cleveland sent a ragtag team of doctors and dentists into his mouth, to steal a bunch of cancer.

He assembled his band of skilled and trustworthy specialists and scheduled a top-secret cancer heist/surgery. Oh, and to make sure the media didn't follow up, he arranged for the whole thing to take place *on a fucking boat*. He told no one but the men performing his surgery, the ship's captain, and Daniel Lamont, his secretary of war. He didn't even tell his vice president, the man who would assume the presidency should Cleveland die during his mysterious boat surgery.

On July 1, 1893, the standing president of the United States was sedated by nitrous oxide and ether, strapped into a chair anchored to the mast of a ship in the middle of the ocean, and received major surgery. Only about twelve people in the world knew about it; everyone else just thought the president was enjoying his Fourth of July weekend at sea (which, of course, is exactly what devious ol' Cleveland *wanted* them to think). The already-risky surgery was made even more dangerous by being at sea (which is why most doctors today rarely suggest getting mouth-cancer surgery on a boat). The doctors cut into Cleveland's face and into his sinuses—making sure all of the incisions happened inside the president's mouth, so as not to leave a visible scar—and removed a "gelatinous mound" of cancer. And, yeah, cancer comes in "gelatinous mounds," because *gross*, right? Cancer sucks so much.

The secret procedure was a success, and the country didn't even find out about it until decades later, nine years after Cleveland's

GROVER'S 11

death. Sure, the dentist who helped perform the surgery went public with the information as soon as it was clear that the president was going to be in good health. He believed the danger had passed, but when he tried to share the story with the world, the White House aggressively and categorically denied his claims. The dentist was ridiculed and ostracized as a liar.

See, being president changes a man. It turned honest Grover, a man who paid child support for a kid who probably wasn't even his, into a man who betrayed the public trust he claimed to hold so sacred. Be on guard. He'll talk a big fat game about how honest and decent he is, but if his back is against the wall, there's no *telling* what he'll resort to.

Also, watch out for him because, even without his deviousness, Cleveland was terrifying. As a child, he wasn't just talking eloquently about how to "become a great man"; he was also regularly ripping fence posts out of the ground with his bare hands. He was 5'11" and 250 lbs of president and his fists were described as "ham-like," which might be delicious but is probably just scary and painful. He loved hunting and often carried around a rifle that he nicknamed "Death and Destruction," which isn't a nickname a rifle earns for being *pretty.*

Still, as big and ham-fisted and bacon-fingered as he was, and as tough as he looked, Cleveland wasn't in a shape anyone would call "good" (he was, in fact, more of a gelatinous mound of a man than anything else). Apparently he stopped that fence-post-ripping shit as soon as he hit puberty. Cleveland loathed exercise and once said, "Bodily movement alone is among the dreary and unsatisfying things of life." If you've ever worked out even a *little* bit, you're more prepared for this fight than Cleveland, and almost certainly faster. Aim for his jaw, avoid his rifle, and if you knock him down, stick around for a while to make *sure* he's down. Like a horror movie serial killer, Cleveland was *notorious* for his ability to surprise everyone and come back as soon as they thought he was down for the count.

BENJAMIN HARRISON:

THE HUMAN ICEBERG

★ ★ ★

enjamin Harrison is not to be fucked with. He was quick, stocky, and efficient with his actions, and according to historian William DeGregorio, he "tackled problems through mastery of detail." Harrison was a man who, when convinced of his own rightness, was completely immovable (this, in conjunction with his cold nature, earned him the nickname the "Human Iceberg," although I also have a pet theory that it's because he singlehandedly sunk the *Titanic* with a head-butt). Harrison's rigid and stern nature (he was described by Theodore Roosevelt as "cold-blooded") applied to his schoolyard fights, his politics, and, presumably, his cage matches with time travelers.

Unfortunately for anyone who has ever come up against him, Harrison was *always* convinced of his own rightness, thanks to his deep and personal relationship with religion. A devout Presbyterian, Harrison was a former deacon and Sunday school teacher and, as president, was so serious about his religion that he conducted no political business on Sundays. When he won the election, the first words out of his mouth were "Now I walk with God."

You want to know the most terrifying kind of person? It's the guy with a military background given absolute power who sincerely believes he was elected God's friend. That's a confidence that's almost impossible to match. It was also a huge leap, because there's some compelling evidence that Harrison's win wasn't exactly legitimate. He lost the popular vote to incumbent president Cleveland, and only won the electoral votes from New York (Cleveland's home state) because the party bosses that ran New York were furious with Cleveland's honesty and his reform efforts. The bosses wanted to punish Cleveland, so they got together, raised some money, and (possibly) stole the election for Harrison (when Harrison credited his victory to God in front of Matthew Quay, one of the bosses who ensured victory, Quay reportedly said "Then let God reelect you" before storming out of the president's sight). Even though all evidence was pointing toward shady corruption, Harrison wanted to believe that God made him president, and nothing was going to shake him of that belief.

That's not to say that Harrison's supreme self-confidence in his badassedness wasn't *completely* bullshit. In 1862, Harrison raised the 70th Indiana Infantry and served as their colonel in the Civil War. Even though he hadn't had military experience at the time, the governor of Indiana had to beg him *twice* to become a colonel for the infantry, because he simply radiated the kind of ass-kicking ass-kickery that you look for in a colonel. Harrison eventually accepted his command position and, even though he was a strict disciplinarian (he accepted only the best from himself and therefore wouldn't tolerate anything less from anyone else), he earned the admiration of the soldiers he commanded with his bravery and courage. While he later admitted to not enjoying the war (he claimed he'd prefer to have breakfast instead of a fight, which, sure, if *those* are your choices, obviously), he was just as thorough and calculating on the battlefield as he was anywhere else, and just as uncompromising.

As president, Harrison embodied the kind of "America as Global Bully" stereotype that other presidents before and since have always tried to downplay. Harrison wanted America to be *bigger* (he added North and South Dakota, Montana, Washington, Idaho, and Wyoming into the Union), he wanted it to be *stronger* (he spent money building up the navy and strengthening our military), and he wanted the rest of the world to recognize and fear the tremendous balls that America swung with such gusto and reckless pride. When Canadian ships started fishing in areas that Harrison believed to belong to America, he had the ships and the crews taken prisoner. When he saw Hawaii, he decided "I want that," and sent in American troops to overthrow the current Hawaiian Queen in a coup. Remember, Harrison was a man who believed he was right *and* God's buddy, so if

he wanted your ships or your tropical island paradise, he was going to *take it.*

When Harrison couldn't get as much done in America as he'd wanted, he turned outward to the rest of the world to leave his mark. Harrison's intense patriotism (a good quality to have in a president), and his bullish toughness (a *terrifying* one), meant that he would never back down from a fight, especially if it involved another country. During his presidency, two American sailors got into a fight and died in a saloon brawl in Valparaíso, Chile. It wasn't an act of aggression from Chile as a nation; it was just a saloon fight, and the Chilean minister of foreign affairs assured Harrison that he was handling the situation as he handled every disruption of the law in Chile. Still, Harrison wouldn't stand for it and told Chile that if they didn't immediately and publicly apologize and pay some form of restitution for the two deceased sailors, *he would go to war.* The minister eventually apologized and paid $75,000, because the guy who threatens to send his constantly expanding navy to war after the accidental deaths of two men is *not* a man that you try to reason with. Later, the roles were reversed: a number of Italian immigrants were lynched in New Orleans and the leader of Italy similarly demanded an apology. Harrison refused to apologize, accused Italy of overreacting based on absolutely nothing, and threatened *them* with war. No one fucks with America on Harrison's watch, not even people who aren't technically trying to fuck with America.

Harrison isn't just eager to start a fight; he also knows how to win one. Late one night, a deranged man broke through a window into the White House with a belly full of liquor and a strong desire to kill President Harrison (this is the worst kind of drunk to be). Armed with beer muscles that granted him a low tolerance for pain and a ton of general madness, the attacker was able to subdue the *two men* who tried to take him down. Two doormen tried to double-team the invading drunk, but they were simply no match for his passion and whiskey punches. Harrison (who got out of bed and moved to action as soon as he heard a window break), burst into the room where the drunk lunatic was and singlehandedly took him down and pinned both of his arms at his sides so hard that one of the doormen likened Harrison's grip to that of a vise. With the man still pinned motionless, Harrison calmly asked the two White House staffers what else he could do for them, and one sheepishly replied that he could maybe cut down one of the window cords and use it to tie the intruder up. Harrison did it quickly and then handed the man over to the police. He didn't do this as some young spring chicken in the war, but as a crotchety, beardy president in his late fifties.

When you fight Harrison, remember that he, as a deeply religious man, is going to tag-team you with God as his ring mate. If he raises his fists to you, chances are that he believes God has specifically chosen him to do it, in which case, *fuck,* watch out. He stayed in good shape his whole life and has no clear physical weaknesses, so you just have to hold out hope that his pride will get the better of him. Or just grab him by the beard and tug on it. He was the last president to wear a beard; make him regret it.

WILLIAM McKINLEY

IS BIG, MAD, AND HUNGRY AS HELL

★ ★ ★

Remember when we said Buchanan was badass for smoking twenty cigars a day? William "The Major" McKinley smoked cigars too, but he also *straight-up ate them*. There's only one other person I know of who regularly ate cigars (Apone, from the movie *Aliens*), and he lit giant space monsters on fire for a living.

Is it fair to assume that Apone was based on Big Bill? Historians remain divided, but yes, yes it is fair.

McKinley volunteered for service in the Civil War at eighteen years old. At the time, he was weak and sickly and had no combat or fighting experience, so he was put to work in the commissary. The kitchen might not seem like the most badass place to be in a war, but McKinley made it work; he earned distinction and respect for running right to the frontlines to make sure all of the soldiers had food and water, taking enemy fire the whole time. He regularly wrote in his diary that he knew he would probably die soon, but he wasn't nervous or afraid, because he knew he was serving his country (and literally serving his countrymen) and would die doing what he believed in, showing the kind of nobility that would make a *modern* eighteen-year-old shit himself. McKinley was so good at feeding people and not dying that he was quickly promoted several times, eventually earning the rank and nickname "The Major." His commander, Rutherford B. Hayes, said that McKinley showed "unusual and unsurpassed capacity." He entered service weak and pale, but he left after four years looking strong, healthy, and confident.

As a man and a president, McKinley never made any decisions without carefully thinking through every issue from every angle. During his presidency, there was a lot of pressure from both his own cabinet and sensationalist journalists like Joseph Pulitzer and William Randolph Hearst to get America involved in Cuba's war for independence from Spain. Hearst and Pulitzer worked Americans into a frenzy with their ridiculous and exaggerated tales of Spanish savagery, and it seemed like everyone in the country was begging for war, but McKinley wouldn't be moved by newspapermen. He had already lived through a war, he'd seen bodies pile up, and he treated military aggression like an absolute last resort. Critics unfairly accused McKinley of suffering from indecision, but really he was just thoughtful. He only got America involved after he'd exhausted every available diplomatic solution, and when he *did* get us involved, he got us *the fuck* involved.

McKinley went from being against the Spanish-American War to being an incredibly competent and decisive wartime commander in chief. He converted a room of the White House into a war room and was directly connected to just about every commander in the field, checking in with soldiers by phone several times a day. His mastery of detail and his military experience made him an incredibly efficient commander; the Spanish-American War ended in just four months, with more American casualties the result of disease than of actual attack. It was an important war, because it established America as a global superpower and it let Americans see Northerners, Southern-

ers, blacks, and whites all fighting together for a noble cause (some-thing Americans, still dealing with the aftermath of the Civil War, desperately needed to see). America even got control of the Philip-pines after the war, and *we didn't even want it.*

Unless you're a terrible asshole, it'll be tough to fight McKinley, not just because he's big and strong and experienced, but because he was a *super* nice and likable guy. He was polite, gave everyone the benefit of the doubt, and Democrats and Republicans alike were charmed by him, and he was just the greatest husband ever. McKin-ley's devotion to his wife was legendary in DC. As governor of Ohio, McKinley made sure that his office was across the street from his home. This was because, every single day at three o'clock, it was important for him to stop what he was doing, go to his window, and give his wife, Ida, a simple wave (she would stand in the window of their home and wave back). Even though they had breakfast together every morning, and even though he *also* waved to her from across the street right before he entered his office.

As president, McKinley broke protocol by having his wife sit next to him during official White House dinners (it was custom at the time for the First Lady to sit with the guest of honor, *across* from, but not next to, the president). He did this because she had epilepsy and was prone to seizures, and if he sensed one coming on during dinner, he would cover Ida's face with a napkin or cloth, to spare her the embarrassment of having people watch her face twitch and contort. When the attack passed, he'd remove the napkin and move on as if nothing had happened.

He's a *super-sweet guy,* and now you have to fight him, and that sucks, because he'll probably give you a gift or something right before the fight starts. You can only hope that luck is on your side, and that's not just bullshit—luck could really play an important role in this. McKinley wore a red carnation every day as a good luck charm, and because it pleased his wife. One day, minutes after he removed his lucky carnation and gave it to a young girl as a present (*such a sweet guy*), he was shot by a deranged anarchist named Leon Czolgosz, and even *that guy* got a pass from McKinley. McKinley's first words after being shot were "Don't let them hurt him" (upon seeing his assassin tackled to the ground) and "My wife, be careful . . . how you tell her—oh, be careful." His immediate concern was for his killer and his wife, and how she would take the news of his attack.

His kindness was not rewarded. When McKinley got to the hospital, there was no doctor around who could perform surgery except one, a gynecologist who couldn't find the bullet. Despite the best efforts of one of Buffalo's finest vagina doctors, McKinley died on September 12, 1901, eight days after being shot.

So, if McKinley has his lucky flower, you just might be screwed. This is a man who is confident in his convictions and is prepared to die defending them, a man who doesn't even need luck to win in his fight against you, but still might have it. Also, *so* sweet. Even if you *were* stronger and luckier than McKinley, you should let him win anyway. Think of his wife, man. Don't be a dick.

TEDDY ROOSEVELT

WILL SPEAK SOFTLY AND

BEAT THE SHIT OUT OF YOU

★ ★ ★

If you're anything like me, you wrote an entire book about presidents as a flimsy excuse to talk about how much you love Theodore Roosevelt. If anything in this chapter is misspelled it's because it's almost impossible to type with a massive, Roosevelt-induced erection. Okay. Here we go.

It's hard to imagine that TR, without question the most badass president we have ever had or will ever have, was once sickly. Indeed, throughout his childhood, he was almost always on the verge of death. He complained of upset stomachs, headaches, asthma, and wrote in his journal that "nobody seemed to think [he] would live." When most kids are as perpetually sick as Roosevelt was, they get babied by their parents, but TR's folks knew they were raising a steel-shitting cowboy-in-training, and they treated him as such from day one. When Lil' TR's asthma acted up, his dad gave him a cigar to smoke and his mother rubbed his chest so hard that he spit up blood. Roosevelt's dad, who wanted TR to toughen up, told him on his fourteenth birthday that he had "the mind but . . . not the body, and without the help of the body, the mind cannot go as far as it should." TR said simply, "I'll make my body."

And ho. Lee. Shit. He did.

TR took up boxing. And wrestling. And hunting. And running. And fighting. Gradually, he beat his sickness, even his asthma, making him the only human in history to intimidate asthma into submission (though, really, can you blame the asthma?). TR wasn't satisfied with just getting stronger and overcoming his illnesses; he wanted to beat everything. He consciously forced himself to take whatever path seemed harshest and most dangerous, surrounding himself with whatever inspired the most terror *(like Batman, you guys).*

TR summed up his life philosophy and his fear-immersive approach to life simply: "Man does in fact become fearless by sheer dint of practicing fearlessness." That, ladies and gentlemen, is the most Rooseveltian sentence ever written.

Going through Roosevelt's resume is like reading a how-to guide on ass-kicking manliness. He was a cattle rancher, a deputy sheriff, an explorer, a police commissioner, the assistant secretary of the navy, the governor of New York, and a war hero. Also, a full-on cowboy. TR's mother and wife died on the exact same day, and while some people take a blow like that and just lock themselves up in a room and cry for days, Teddy, like the Eastwoodian badass that he was *(or like a Batman)*, left his home behind and moved out to a wild and untamed area. In TR's case, this meant going West to work as a cowboy, catching, riding, and branding horses and bulls and, occasionally, kicking some stray ass that got out of line. Once, he was tired after a long day of cowboying so he entered a saloon to catch a drink and some rest. An unruly cowboy (with a cocked gun in each hand) made fun of TR, calling him "Four Eyes" and demanding that he buy everyone in the saloon a drink. TR tried ignoring him, but when the cowboy persisted, TR gave the armed moron three quick punches to the face. The man was knocked unconscious and, as soon as he woke up the next morning, left town, never to be seen again, because maybe he never stopped running. They say that, on quiet nights if you listen closely, you can still hear him pissing himself.

On another occasion, TR was fox hunting with some friends and almost *everyone* lost their shit that day (fox hunting used to be *crazy* dangerous). One dislocated his knee, one broke several ribs, another got half of his face ripped off by what must have been the most pissed-off fox in the forest, and TR himself got knocked off his horse, landed on a pile of stones, and then got crushed by his own horse. His face was covered with blood, his left wrist was fractured, but he got back on the horse and continued to ride and hunt for five miles. The next day he went for a three-hour walk.

This is just a shot in the dark, because I don't know you personally, but I'm guessing you don't have a similarly badass story under your belt.

Out of all of his jobs, hobbies, and passions, Roosevelt always had a special spot in his heart for unadulterated violence. He talked about fighting the way poets talked about love, saying once that every man "who has in him any real power of joy in battle knows that he feels it when the wolf begins to rise in his heart; he does not then shrink from blood or sweat or deem that they mar the fight; he revels in them, in the toil, the pain, and the danger, as but setting off the triumph." I know you have to fight this man, and that's probably weighing heavily on you right now, but please take a second to appreciate just how *beautiful* and *eloquent* TR can get when it comes to beating the shit out of people.

Roosevelt was always praying for a chance to serve in a war, and in 1898 he got his wish when America intervened in a dispute between Spain and Cuba. TR quickly formed the first U.S. Volunteer Cavalry regiment, a group of cowboys and fighters that he called the Rough Riders. They were one of the first groups in the war, all because Roosevelt pushed them hard, saying "It will be awful if we miss the fun," because Roosevelt and I have very different ideas of fun. Most people already know of the Rough Riders and their historic charge up San Juan Hill, but few know that, since their horses had to be left behind, the Riders made this charge entirely on foot. Whenever it looked like someone might retreat, Roosevelt threatened to shoot them, saying he "always kept his promises." Most of his troops laughed, saying "Ha ha, that's true," and continued fighting, all laughing together about how crazy Roosevelt was. You just could not stop this man from violencing the hell out of a San Juan Hill.

Don't think that Roosevelt lost his obsession with violence when he became president. Don't you dare *ever* think that. TR strolled through the White House with a pistol on his person at all times, though, with his black belt in jujitsu and his history as a champion boxer, it wasn't like he really needed it. It wasn't just his war record or the fact that he knew several different ways to kill you that made Roosevelt such a badass. It wasn't even the fact that he kept a bear and a lion at the White House as pets (though that certainly helps). Teddy Roosevelt was a badass of the people. Roosevelt received letters from army cavalrymen complaining about having to ride twenty-five miles a day for training and, in response, Teddy rode horseback for a hundred miles, from sunrise to sunset, at fifty-one years old, *while president,* effectively removing anyone's right to complain about anything, ever again.

Roosevelt was never injured in any of the battles he fought, but while campaigning for a third term, he was shot by a madman. Instead of treating the wound, Roosevelt delivered his campaign speech with the bleeding, undressed bullet hole in his chest. Even though he said he would take it easy on this speech given the circumstances, he spoke for *an hour and a half.* Right before addressing his crowd, Roosevelt opened his coat, revealed the bleeding wound to the crowd, and said, "The bullet is in me now." He then unzipped his pants, pulled out his dick, and said, "And now check *this* out. Pretty rad, right? Guy tried to shoot me here and the bullets bounced right off, swear to God. Who's got a gun? Someone try to shoot ol' Teddy in the dick, see what happens."

(Probably.)

Some presidents, upon leaving the White House, return to law or enjoy retirement peacefully, or write books. Roosevelt went on African safaris and killed elephants, because *who was going to stop him.*

Asthma, partial blindness, the Spanish Army, bullets, and death couldn't take down old Teddy. But, hey, now it's your turn! Honestly, the only way you could hope to have any chance whatsoever against Roosevelt is if you can somehow out-Roosevelt him. By teaching you how to master fearlessness, he has *given you the tools* to defeat him. Can you do it? Can you immerse yourself in fear and make fear your cowering bitch, as Roosevelt did? Can you overcome every one of your failings and insecurities and rise above? Can you take down the man who famously urged men to "speak softly and carry a big stick," even though he personally shouted constantly and wielded pistols? *Can you out-Roosevelt Roosevelt?*

Hey. Spoiler alert: No.

WILLIAM "THE EATIN' CRETIN" TAFT

WILL DEVOUR THE COMPETITION, AND 27 OTHER FAT JOKES

★ ★ ★

Maxing out at 340 lbs, William Howard Taft has the distinction of being not only our fattest president, but—wait, nope, that's it. FATTEST PRESIDENT. It's on his tombstone and everything (and if it isn't, I'm going to personally add it sometime in the future).

Taft's presidency is mostly (unfortunately) remembered for how average it was. He followed Teddy Roosevelt, and even though Taft's big fat giant feet could utterly annihilate Roosevelt's literal shoes, Taft was never really a big enough man to fill them metaphorically. Roosevelt was a man who believed the president could and should do anything he wanted (unless the law explicitly said not to), and Taft was a lawman who thought the president could *only* do what was explicitly written in the Constitution. As a result, Taft's administration was full of a lot of important reforms, but it lost the exciting sexiness of Roosevelt's terms. His staunch by-the-book-ness earned Taft the ire of Roosevelt, and presumably, like so many pairs of presidential pants, Taft almost ripped the Republican Party apart completely.

Did this upset Taft? Not really. In a lot of ways, Taft was one of the saner men to serve as president because, unlike almost everyone else in this book, Taft really, *really* didn't want to be the president. Taft loved the law and wanted to be a chief justice of the Supreme Court, as that's where his talents and interests lay. He only accepted the nomination in the first place because his ambitious wife wanted him to, and because Teddy Roosevelt had handpicked Taft as his successor, and when Teddy Roosevelt tells you to do something, you goddamn *do it* or risk having him punch you in the butt so hard your poop stays inside you forever out of fear of possibly running into Roosevelt.

Taft wasn't exactly a do-nothing president; he really got rid of some dead weight in the Treasury Department and trimmed a lot of fat out of the military budget and busted a lot of bloated trusts and, in fact, the only time he broke a reduction-related promise was when he vowed to the American people that he'd lose thirty pounds while in the White House (he in fact gained quite a bit). That is a true fact, it's not a fat joke. If you turned to this chapter looking for cheap fat jokes, well . . . just hang on for a few more paragraphs.

Taft eventually *did* excel at a job when Warren Harding finally named him chief justice of the Supreme Court after he'd left the White House; and serving on the court (the only president ever to do so) is what Taft considered to be the highlight of his life. Taft didn't look back fondly on his presidency, and according to letters he wrote to close friends, he hardly even remembered his time spent in the White House at all.

This is largely because Taft *didn't* spend too much time in the White House. He hated the job so much that he spent most of his time driving around or golfing or just generally avoiding being the president. He was always a big guy, but tended to overeat when he got into the White House, because he was so depressed and food was the only thing that cheered him up. As soon as he left office, he lost eighty pounds and was happier and healthier than he'd been since college. In your fight with Taft, let's hope you get the bloated, presidential, Elvis-at-the-end-of-his-career Taft, and not the fitter, more energized Elvis-at-literally-any-other-time Taft.

Much in the way that he'd never turn down a meal, Taft won't turn down a fight, even if he's not hungry for one. On the subject of punching jerks, Taft has said, "I am a man of peace and I don't want to fight. But when I do fight, I want to hit hard. Even a rat in a corner will fight." He was Yale's intramural heavyweight wrestling champion, so he's got a little more experience than a rat in a corner, but you will likely not be playing by standard Ivy League College Wrestling Rules in your fight, so that could be an advantage for you.

Now, this might sound crazy, but if you want to beat Taft, try to fight him around some bathtubs. This is because William Howard Taft, an adult man, *while president,* once got stuck in a bathtub.

It's a fairly famous story but still one of my all-time favorite stories about presidents and my number-one favorite story about bathtubs. One day, Taft was bathing and was *so big* that he got stuck in the White House bathtub. He sat there for a while stewing, not only in his own considerable juices, but also in the knowledge that, no matter what he did as president or Supreme Court judge, *this* was what he'd be remembered for. He could do whatever he wanted, but at the end of the day, assholes who write books about presidents would still dedicate the bulk of their Taft chapters to this one, stupid, hilarious story.

Taft struggled to wriggle himself free of the tub's clutches, but he knew it was no use. Finally, having abandoned the idea that maybe he could just live in the bathtub forever, Taft called to an aide to help him out. The aide recognized immediately that this wasn't a job for one man and called three of his buddies and the team got Taft out and if they didn't get any medals for doing it without laughing, they damn well should have. Four men. It took four men to extract the president of the Foodnited Tastes from his tub. A new tub was installed just to accommodate the large president, and that's why today we have the Pacific Ocean.

Taft wasn't just hilariously fat, he was also *hilariously fat*. As a result of his considerable weight, Taft had a problem with gas and flatulence (considered by many to be the ghosts of food trying to escape). He would embarrass the rest of his staff by burping and farting too much in front of visiting foreign dignitaries, and if that's not bad enough, *shut up*, you're lying, that's *totally* bad enough. Taft would eat so much that he'd pass out in the middle of meetings and conversations. His body, one assumes, had to make a choice between dedicating its energy to digesting the impossible amount of food Taft ate that day or keeping him awake, and, more often than not, it chose digestion. I don't think it's a coincidence that Big William only has four letters in his last name and three of them are *F-A-T*. Taft loved food so much that, when he took his inaugural oath, he swore on not a Bible, but an IHOP menu. William Taft was so big that he used to trick people into thinking his face was on Mount Rushmore just by standing next to it. President Taft was so big he used the Bible Belt to keep his pants up. William Howard Motherfucking Taft was so big that when he sat around the White House, he sat *around* the White House and then *ate France*.

So, pound for pound (and pound and pound), he's got you beat, and he's clearly got some fight in him, but he's also got enough food to feed all of Delaware in him, so your chances are pretty good. If he gets on top of you or suspects for even a second that any part of you is made of ham, you won't stand a chance.

WOODROW WILSON

WILL CLAIM TO "KEEP YOU OUT OF PAIN" AND THEN TOTALLY PUT YOU IN PAIN

★ ★ ★

Thomas Woodrow Wilson is the only person in history to have a PhD *and* the presidency *and* a Nobel Peace Prize under his belt. He was also dyslexic, blind in one eye, and didn't learn to read until age ten, which should tell you the most important lesson you need to learn about Wilson: if he wants something, he's going to go for it. In his first term alone, he made more reforms and had more laws passed—including the Federal Reserve Act, child labor laws, and the creation of the Federal Trade Commission—than almost any other president before or since. It was on his watch that women were given the right to vote and workers were given the right to not work so many hours in a single day that they die.

The other important lesson you need to learn about Wilson is that he was just a walking sack of death. In addition to the previously mentioned partial blindness, he also suffered constant crushing headaches that never went away, and lived with recurring stomach pain that was so bad he traveled with his own stomach pump, which he used on himself every single day at the suggestion of a shitty physician until a White House doctor said, *"Who told you to do that? HOLY SHIT STOP THAT."* He had writer's cramp in his right hand and stabbing pains in his left shoulder and leg, and lived through what many medical historians refer to as "just a *buttload* of strokes."

His already shaky health was tested even more in his second term, which Wilson devoted to the League of Nations. Wilson proudly kept America out of World War I in his first term, but when Germany refused to stop attacking American ships, Wilson was forced to declare war and drop the hammer. And drop it he did! Wilson led us into war during his second term and made sure that our soldiers always had food and ammo, and he signed a peace treaty before his term had ended. Seeing peace even in war, Wilson thought of World War I as an opportunity to build the League of Nations, an international super-friends team focused on maintaining global peace *by any means necessary* (diplomacy, usually). At the time, no one else was behind Wilson's idea, and the lack of support just seemed to make him sicker and crazier. Oh, right, the craziness. Wilson was, by his own description, "impulsive, passionate, canny, tenacious, [and] cold," and he once compared himself to a "dormant volcano, placid on the outside, a boiling caldron within." When he pitched his League of Nations to the world only to get laughed at, the lava he kept stored on the inside started to bubble to the surface. He became angry and rude and bitter and his body started falling apart in a really bizarre manner; it started morphing in such a way that it caused his appearance to line up with his inner anger/craziness. The strain of having to deal with uncooperative foreign allies "contracted [Wilson's] usually relaxed facial muscles into sharp ridges of hostility," making him appear "haggard"; he perpetually looked angry and ferocious. Also, that one blind eye started twitching and fluttering like a tiny, round humming bird, trapped in an angry volcano face.

During this time, Wilson was irritable and grew suspicious of even his closest friends (something later historians attributed to undiagnosed brain damage). Wilson went days without sleeping and his brain slowly started deteriorating, which, like everything at this point, only made Wilson angrier and more stubborn. Determined to win public support for the League of Nations, which became his white whale, Wilson decided to, against the orders of his wife, physicians, and basic common sense, tour the country and give speeches to rally the people to his side. He was riding all over America, coughing and sneezing and being fed predigested foods (the only food he could eat) by day, and giving rousing speeches by night (sometimes five before bedtime). He delivered his speeches with closed eyes, shaking hands, and a weakened voice. With his wheezing, his sleeplessness, his strained mumbling, his rapidly failing body, and singularly

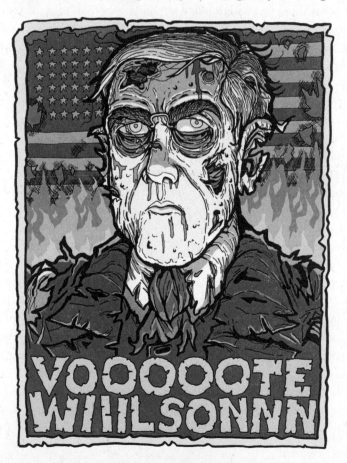

obsessed focus, it's not completely uncalled-for to label Woodrow Wilson our first Zombie President.

After his first stroke, Wilson cut the tour short and went back to the White House to relax, because presidenting is such a cakewalk of a job that we should all do it when we need a vacation.

Here was the problem: the doctors believed that if Wilson stepped down and left the White House, the disgrace and humiliation would kill him, but they also thought that if he actually tried to continue to be president, the *stress* would kill him, because "Hey, I'm a doctor in the early 1900s, I can say whatever I want and no one can stop me." Wilson's health had gotten so bad that he could barely walk, his mind was deteriorating so thoroughly that he could barely make decisions, and his demeanor was getting so nasty that his aides started to resign, one by one, having grown tired of the president's hurtful outbursts and personal attacks.

So . . . who was actually running things?

In 1919, Wilson's second wife, Edith, became the unofficial president of the United States. She decided which matters would be brought to Wilson and which ones would be thrown out. She secretly presided over the country while Wilson, her Crypt Keeper of a husband and president, got sicker, crazier, and angrier. This was kept far out of the public eye (people back then were, as people today, very much against the idea of a mummy being president).

All that said, don't feel bad about fighting him, even though punching him will probably feel like hitting a helpless old man who has pneumonia instead of bones. Wilson did a lot of good for America, but he also earns distinction for being one of our country's most racist presidents, and he wasn't even one of the presidents who personally owned slaves. Most of *those* guys were *less* racist than Wilson. Wilson's administration sought to increase the amount of segregationists and decrease the amount of black people in office, and he even segregated federal government offices, something that hadn't been done since the mid-1800s. It could be argued that Wilson was from a different time, but it could *also* be argued that *so was Lincoln, you asshole.*

Keep all of this in mind when you enter the cage or ring or Thunderdome with the twenty-eighth president of the United States, Woodrow Wilson. Focus on how much of a racist he is, and that should make your punches and kicks feel a little more satisfying. Remember how driven he was, parading himself around as president for a few years even though he was basically a bag of farts and racist death wails two months into his second term, and remember how full of rage and boiling lava he was. Also remember that he is just a time bomb of illness and weird body shit. Try to avoid letting him sneeze on, cough on, breathe on, or look at you, at all costs.

WARREN G. HARDING

IS DESPERATE TO PROVE
HE'S GOOD AT SOMETHING

★ ★ ★

Historians often like to point out how easy it is to ridicule twenty-ninth president of the United States Warren G. Harding for his spectacular failures as a pathetic worm of a president, but they neglect to mention that it's also incredibly fun and very justified. Harding is one of the most consistently hated and shat-upon presidents in the history of both politics *and* shitting. Throughout his life, enemies, friends, family members, and voters walked all over Harding and every time he just *took* it, sitting idly by while members of his cabinet royally ripped off America in scandal after scandal. The first time he tried to speak in front of a large gathering of Republicans, his own party *booed him*. Roosevelt's daughter called him a "slob" *for no clear reason*. His miserable presidency was so full of bad decisions, you'd think it was a high school date-rape ad. And he just took it all with a smile and a "Thank you, sir, may I have another?"

The only president who ranks lower than Harding on any poll is William Henry Harrison, and that's because Harrison died thirty days into his term. All Harding had to do to be better was live slightly longer, which he did, but that was *it*. He gave cushy government jobs to all of his longtime friends, who swiftly and efficiently learned how to illegally make massive amounts of money off of the trust of the American people. He made his friend Albert Fall the secretary of the interior; Fall was later arrested for accepting bribes in exchange for selling American oil fields to personal business associates. This came to be known as the Teapot Dome Scandal, and it was just the most famous of the scandals to rock the Harding administration, not the *only* one. The head of the Office of Alien Property *and* the head of the Justice Department were *also* convicted of accepting bribes, and the head of the Veterans Bureau skimmed profits and organized a small, underground drug ring (which, yes, is a *supervillainesque* level of evil).

One of Harding's smartest career moves was quietly dying in office while traveling around the country in 1923. He had an enlarged heart, but not the kind that the Grinch had, the kind that kills shitty presidents. Mysterious circumstances surrounded his death, but no autopsy was performed, presumably because the coroners figured that if he was poisoned, he was sort of asking for it.

It is specifically this rich history of straight-up "taking it" that makes Harding a ticking time bomb. Don't confuse Harding's ineptitude as a political leader with an inability to handle himself in a fight. Harding, for all of his many faults, was very calculating and *sneaky*. He liked to put up a front as a softie and a gentleman while surreptitiously advancing his own agenda in the background, as he did in 1884 when he acquired the *Marion Star*, a sinking ship of a newspaper in Ohio with only seven hundred subscribers. With Harding at the helm, the *Star* quickly surpassed its competitors. Some people credited shrewd business practices, or the goodwill Harding had built up in the community, but Harding's charm and likability were just a distraction. The *Star* succeeded because Harding trashed the everloving shit out of the name of his paper's biggest competitor, the

Marion Independent. According to Harding scholar Robert K. Murray, in his public and private life Harding the man always seemed to have an "amiable and genial personality"—which is why it came as such a shock when his paper started charging the competing *Independent*'s owner "with being 'a liar,' 'a lickspittle,' 'a moral leper,' and 'a disgruntled and disappointed old ass.'"

Whether or not the owner was, in fact a "lickspittle," and whether or not such a word was ever even a thing, is all lost to history. The bottom line is it worked and the *Independent* collapsed under the might of the ballsy, tough-as-nails *Star.* Harding later used the influence of his paper to launch his political career and attract the attention of the Republican Party.

As a politician, Harding didn't really have any policies about which he felt passionate, he just *wanted* the presidency so badly, it didn't matter what he had to say or do to get there. He had a track record of voting based on what he thought was going to *win,* regardless of whether or not he thought he was voting for the *right* side. It wasn't about morals, it was about backing the right horse to avoid being left behind. He didn't want to help the nation or create jobs or change the world, he just wanted a position of power and was determined to get it. At any cost.

Harding's strategy of presenting a sweet and unassuming front while aggressively backdooring his way into getting what he wants can be seen in everything he ever did. It was widely believed, for example, that Harding's wife, Florence, ran the house while the timid, doting Harding trailed behind with his head lowered and his tail between his legs; yet nothing could be further from the truth. It was in 1905, right around the time Harding had successfully nailed the obedient puppy dog act, when he started nailing something else: a young Ohio woman named Carrie Phillips.

While plenty of presidents have had affairs, Harding's is probably the sneakiest and sleaziest. Harding began his affair in the spring of '05, while Mrs. Harding was in Columbus "undergoing treatment for a kidney ailment" and Carrie's husband, James, a longtime friend of Harding's, was "soothing his nerves at the Battle Creek Sanitarium."

He had an *additional* affair years later with someone thirty years his junior, but even that not-insignificant level of sleaziness doesn't top the original. Having an affair with your good friend's wife while he's in an institution and *your* wife is in a hospital ranks you somewhere between Benedict Arnold and the guy who invented *Girls Gone Wild* on the spectrum of Total Dickheads in American History.

Right before the Republican Party decided to nominate Harding for the presidency, they asked him to search his soul and come clean with any skeletons in his closet. He spent ten minutes investigating his conscience before calmly and confidently saying, "Nope. Nothing." Minutes later, he was nominated. In 1920, we made him the twenty-ninth president of the United States. Years after his first but not before his last affair.

Notice the patterns? Harding wants you to think he's a nice gentleman, but he'll crush your newspaper and destroy your reputation if you stand in his way. He'll appear to be the faithful, doting husband but cheat with the nearest available chick the second his wife has her back turned (or, alternately, is face-up receiving risky medical treatment for her kidney infection), and will have no problem lying about it to his party when they ask if there are any skeletons in his closet. He has no morals to cling to, no honor. He'll lie to anyone if telling the truth would interfere with his sneaky plans.

Historians like to point out that Harding as a president wasn't corrupt, he just had the misfortune of having terrible friends, but make no mistake, there is a *reason* all of those awful people gravitated toward Harding to begin with. Evil attracts more evil. Carrie, a woman to whom Harding wrote several passionate love letters, was a *freaking Nazi sympathizer,* for Christ's sake.

If you're going to fight Harding, make sure you never turn your back on him. The second he looks wounded and you let your guard down, he'll be up and throwing sand in your eyes faster than you can say "Maybe if you weren't so busy nailing nineteen-year-olds who weren't your wife you wouldn't have let our country fall to shit."

Which, admittedly, isn't very fast considering how long that sentence is, but my point remains: Warren G. Harding sucks.

CALVIN COOLIDGE:

THE SILENT KILLER

★ ★ ★

There's no real way to sugarcoat this: John Calvin Coolidge's biography reads like the chilling origin story of a serial killer. Even the nickname Silent Cal, assigned to the man due to his being famously shy and quiet, calls to mind visions of some creepy, looming bedside murderer. But Silent Cal grew up to be the thirtieth president of the United States, and *not* some kind of eerily quiet murderer who stalked campgrounds.

Probably.

Like a lot of kids, Coolidge was told at an early age that he was not allowed to make mistakes. Unlike a lot of kids, he was often reminded by his parents that he was never going to be the smartest or strongest in his class, so he had better work harder than anyone so he could be the *best*. Coolidge followed his orders and worked harder than anyone and ended up really excelling in school. Is this because he was a good kid who wanted nothing more than to please his folks?

No. It's because, on the rare occasions when he did make a mistake (say, by being late for school), he would be banished to a cold attic, empty but for cobwebs, where he would sit in the dark and wait. For *hours*.

His father, while stern and terrifying, was often away on business, so Coolidge was primarily raised by his grandmother (also stern and terrifying; she was the one who locked him in the attic). People called Coolidge "Silent Cal" because he rarely spoke, but few realize that, even into his presidency, he spoke at length to his mother. Or, rather, his *dead* mother, who passed away when he was twelve. He revealed this in letters to his father, who never responded to the admission (Coolidge's dead mother also refused to comment).

Still, even though he lost his mother and should have been al-lowed some time to grieve, Coolidge continued on his quest to be the best. He just stayed focused and worked hard. Two years later, he lost his fourteen-year-old sister, Abbie. Despite that, and even though he regularly wrote letters to his father talking about how miserable and lonely he was (also unanswered), Coolidge kept on keeping on. He went on to excel in college, law school, and the office of governor of Massachusetts because, make no mistake, he would make no mistakes. He was conditioned to believe a terrifying attic was lurking behind every mistake, and he was *not* going back. So all of that stress and all of that grief and all of that tension was kept balled up inside.

Now, I don't throw the term "Norman Batesian" around a lot, especially when talking about presidents, but a repressed childhood and long conversations with a dead mother? Silent Cal was, without question, the most Norman Batesian man who ever ran this country. First as vice president and then as president. After the corruption-filled shit-show that was the Harding administration, it was up to Coolidge to assure the people that order and integrity had been re-stored to the White House. He needed to convince everyone that a coolheaded and honest man was running the country, and he did.

For a little while.

Then, a few years into his presidency, Coolidge had to watch his sixteen-year-old son, Calvin Jr., die in a freak tennis accident (he stubbed his toe playing tennis, the toe got infected, the infection killed him). This was, we can say, the final tragic straw that broke Coolidge. Tragedy and death followed him everywhere, but unlike Jackson, who ate and subsequently derived tremendous strength from death, Coolidge dwelled on it with the morbid obsession of a Zodiac Killer. He had the Secret Service regularly bring him young boys, just so he could still feel connected to his son in some way (he requested no other guests; just wave after wave of surrogate Calvin Juniors). He could only talk, think, and write about his departed son, mentioning the passing of his son to every White House guest, *as if they somehow hadn't heard*.

Calvin Jr.'s death destroyed Coolidge and his presidency. When Junior was alive, Coolidge was the dynamic and progressive president who made demands of Congress and proudly boasted to his father that "men do what I tell them to do." After Junior died, he was the president who rarely spoke to Congress (or anyone else), got almost nothing done, and stayed inside all day, napping.

Or, not *just* napping. Occasionally, he would take some time to be emotionally distant to his wife and flip out on his staff. This was a man, remember, who was surrounded by tragedy but kept all of his frustrations and heartbreak locked up inside, because he never wanted to let down his stern, distant father by showing that he was anything less than perfect. No one can keep that kind of rage at bay forever; Coolidge was a time bomb, tick, tick, ticking away.

Coolidge kept the White House staff, according to some employees, in a "constant state of anxiety," and was capable of "volcanic eruptions of temper." One White House employee said that "those who saw Coolidge in a rage were simply startled," and that Teddy Roosevelt, "in his worst temper . . . was calm compared with Coolidge." Teddy Roosevelt got his face on Mount Rushmore simply by head-butting the mountain (probably), and Coolidge at his craziest made Teddy look like a *pussycat*.

Still, Coolidge's story isn't *just* about horrible tragedy and premature death. He was also just really weird, in a general sort of way,

and might have been part-Tarzan. He had a pet hippo that he often visited at DC's National Zoo and was frequently seen walking around the White House followed by wild animals, including a pet raccoon, which often would cling to his neck.

But the chief business of fighting Coolidge is *fighting*. Coolidge did not serve in the military and didn't get into any fights as a child. He wasn't really interested in sports, and probably the most exercise he ever got was walking around and window shopping (a favorite pastime of his). He was also sick a lot, with asthma and a chronic cough, both of which forced him to take a number of pills every day.

So, really, if you keep yourself even *slightly* active you might have an advantage. Physically.

Really, all he has on you in this fight is his severe and volcanic rage and an innate ability to control animals.

Be careful.

HERBERT HOOVER

IS THE RAMBO OF PRESIDENTS

★ ★ ★

If you were looking for a good reason to fear thirty-first president Herbert Hoover, you came to the right place (for this information, and absolutely nothing else). Hoover isn't afraid to die, because he's already died once before, and decided that it wasn't so bad. When Hoover was two, his parents thought he was dead. To be clear, it's not like he was sleeping and they thought he was dead for a few seconds before they woke him up. They found him unresponsive and motionless, suffering through a nasty bout of croup, so they put pennies over his eyes and covered him up with a sheet, as was the custom at the *still* time when people died, and then they pronounced him dead (as is *still* the custom when people die).

He survived, obviously, and he held on to those survival skills. When his father died two years later, Hoover carried on, and when his mother died a few years after that, leaving Hoover as an orphan at nine years old, he just kept surviving. With no parents to either raise or protect him, Hoover quickly fell in with a gang of young Native American boys who taught him how to hunt, use a bow and arrow, and generally survive anywhere in the wild. Two years later, he was sent to live with an uncle in Oregon who raised the young Hoover with slightly edited passages from the Bible. "Turn your cheek," Hoover's uncle instructed, "but if he smites you again then punch him." (For any non–Bible scholars wondering which part wasn't in the Bible, it was the "punch your enemies" part.)

So what happens to a boy whose parents first leave him for dead and then just straight-up leave him? He grows up to be the most self-reliant president we've ever had. He was focused, efficient, and fearless, and expected as much from everyone he encountered, and if they *didn't* match his expectations, he'd leave them behind.

Hoover lived by a simple motto: "Work is life." Hoover never sought power, he just liked to work hard and do good in the world. After earning his way through college via various odd jobs, he landed a position with a gold mining company that led to great fortunes. Once he'd turned some money into lots of money and then lots of money into a *crapload* of money, the way all rich people do, Hoover turned his focus to humanitarian efforts, distributing food and supplies to American troops during World War I.

Having national attention for his humanitarian efforts, Hoover was tasked with meeting with German commanders in the middle of the war to negotiate the bringing of aid to American troops held prisoner behind enemy lines. As is customary with the people who manage but don't actually fight wars, Hoover, his associates, and the German commanders met in a comfortable room and sipped martini after martini while discussing, you know, all of those human lives.

Here's where Hoover gets less infuriating and much cannier. He wasn't going to take a break to have a drink *even when he was supposed to be drinking*. He gave his American associates and the bartender strict orders: no matter what the Germans did, the Americans were going to keep their wits about them. The bartender was instructed to pour only *water* in the American martinis, and save the gin for the Germans. Hoover couldn't just trust the bartender to know which drink was which; he needed a way to distinguish his drinks from the Germans', so he demanded that all of the American drinks be served with an onion garnish (instead of the traditional olive). To avoid suspicion, he assured the Germans that this was simply how Americans took their martinis (though the obvious truth is that he wanted to make sure no German accidentally grabbed the wrong drink, exposing the whole ruse).

The plan worked. The Americans kept their heads about them and negotiated brilliantly, while the Germans got sloppier and sloppier, giving the American negotiators the advantage. As a weird epilogue, the bullshit drink that Hoover threw together on the spot to deceive the Germans actually caught on in America. The Gibson martini (named after the general who accompanied Hoover) is one of our more popular gin drinks. Talk about efficiency. Hoover was so efficient that, even with lives on the line, he decides, "I know I'm only doing this to help my scheme, but I might as well make a dynamite drink and immortalize my friend in the process. Ol' 'Two Birds Hoover,' that's what they'll call me."

(No one ever would.)

Hoover continued his humanitarian work, even making sure to give aid to starving Europeans after the war, and when Calvin Coolidge announced that he wouldn't run for office in the 1928 election, Hoover threw his hat in the ring. It wasn't that he grew up dreaming to be the president; it just seemed like a job that would allow him to do the greatest amount of good for the greatest amount of people. Hoover's stellar reputation ensured an easy, landslide victory. Pretty good win for a guy who died at two.

Hoover wasn't our greatest president, but he was certainly one of our most driven. He rarely took vacations, and any time he wasn't working he was antsy and uncomfortable, distracted by the amount of work that he could and should be getting done. He avoided trips and most hobbies, and it was said that he would eat his entire four-course dinners in eight minutes. It's normal for a president to skip a vacation here or there, but Hoover trained himself to wolf down food as efficiently as possible just so he had *more* time to work.

Hoover did enjoy *some* diversions. Every morning, he would wake up and play a spirited game of "Hooverball." Hooverball is similar to volleyball, except instead of hitting the ball back and forth, players stand on opposite sides of a tall net throwing and catching a ball, and instead of using a soft, bouncy volleyball, they used a ten-pound medicine ball. Hoover would hurl a ten-pound ball at his friends and then either catch or get hit by that same ball when they threw it back. A close friend of the president described it as "more strenuous than either boxing, wrestling, or football," and Hoover played it every single morning.

Despite how beloved and effective he was before his presidency, nothing was going to help Hoover once he took office. Almost immediately after he stepped into the White House, the stock market crashed and he made wrong decision after wrong decision, leading us into the Great Depression. He lost reelection to FDR, and even though he spent the rest of his life committed to public service, nothing would change the fact that, in a lot of minds, Hoover was personally responsible for the Great Depression.

The takeaway from *all* of this is that Herbert Hoover is a survivor. He rose from the fake dead at two years old and never looked back. He started with nothing and became a self-made millionaire in no time, and then parlayed that success into the presidency, being the first man to become president without serving in the military or holding public office, just on the strength of his character. He worked every minute of every day without tiring and wasn't sick for a single day of his presidency. He lived for more years after his presidency than any other president in history at the time, and he gave speeches, formed committees, and wrote books right up to his death.

Just because the country fell apart on his watch doesn't mean Hoover's a pushover. The man is *tough*. You won't win your fight on strength or smarts, but simply by *overwhelming* him. Hurl a rock at him while spitting and screaming insults and charging him as fast as you can. One at a time, Hoover can handle almost anything, but throw a number of problems at him and the man crumbles.

FRANKLIN DELANO ROOSEVELT:

ROLLING THUNDER

★ ★ ★

O h, he's in a wheelchair, how bad can this fight be?" you might find yourself wondering. Oh, you. Oh simple, naïve, stupid, stupid *you*. FDR's charisma, optimism, and foresight got us out of the Depression. His leadership skills eased us out of World War II. His effectiveness as a president got him elected for an unprecedented third term. He swam *several miles daily* despite his paralysis.

And you think *you* can beat him just because you've got *legs*? Who do you think you are, *fear itself*? If not, *you are fucked*.

FDR, one of the top two most Rooseveltian Presidents we've had (so far), was, like his fifth cousin TR, incredibly sick and close to death as a child. His mother was so worried that she kept him out of school and had him educated at home until he was fourteen. She also made him wear a dress for the first five years of his life, which doesn't inform FDR's presidency or personality or fighting style, but it's a really weird thing, and you should know. FDR used to wear dresses as a kid.

Whether he was wearing a dress or pants, FDR constantly suffered from headaches and harsh colds and influenza and pneumonia and chronic sinus trouble and occasional temporary paralysis and polio and whatever else was around. If there was a bad disease in the early 1900s, FDR probably caught it.

Unfortunately for disease, no one told FDR that he was supposed to die, so he never let any of his many illnesses stop him. Whenever he wasn't bedridden, FDR could be found working out, swimming, or boxing, making sure his precious windows of good health were spent on physical improvement. He likely would have grown to be just as strong and imposing as TR (he, after all, saw his cousin as a hero), but then that pesky polio showed up. In 1921, Roosevelt spent a day sailing and fishing, then helped some locals put out a forest fire on his way home, then went for a swim, then jogged a mile. Two days later, he couldn't move his legs and the doctors diagnosed it as polio. FDR's doctors told him he wouldn't be able to walk again, and his mother and friends told him it was time to retire and take life easy.

For anyone else, that would be the end of the story, but we're not dealing with anyone else here. The biggest mistake anyone can ever make is telling Franklin Delano Roosevelt that he can't do something. Through years of rigorous and painful exercise, FDR massaged and worked his leg muscles enough that, with the help of iron braces and canes, he was able to stand and walk again. As far as retirement and "taking it easy" went, FDR decided to become New York's governor, assistant secretary of the navy, and eventually settled into a relaxing career as president for longer than anyone else has ever been president.

FDR's struggle with illness and subsequent metal-filled life are remarkably similar to the story of another great leader who was part robot: Iron Man. FDR, much like Tony Stark, was cocky and arrogant before his life-changing diagnosis, but the years of suffering changed all of that, and he emerged more humble, more fearless, and ready to defend America. Also, FDR wore iron braces and used a wheel-

chair, which, for the purposes of this comparison, is *exactly* like a well-armed robot suit.

Scientifically speaking, being more president than other presidents was in FDR's blood. In addition to Teddy, FDR was related in some way to Ulysses S. Grant, Zachary Taylor, and Winston Churchill, which caused many leading historians to dub FDR "The Voltron of Presidential Badassery" (though there are also some fringe historical groups that prefer the label "The Captain Planet of Political Asskickery"). Whichever label you go with, you can't deny that the collection of ridiculously powerful DNA flowing through FDR's veins made it impossible for him *not* to be a great leader.

FDR inherited the presidency when America was in the worst shape it had been in since the Civil War. Twenty-five percent of American workers were jobless, two million people were homeless, and thirty-two out of forty-eight states had closed their banks. You'd have to be crazy to want to take over the country under those conditions, but Roosevelt was part RoboCop, and *all* crazy, and used to facing uphill battles, so he took the job and went to work immediately, passing massive legislation during his first hundred days in office. FDR's New Deal, he assured the American people, was rescuing the United States from the Great Depression; and, at the time, it certainly seemed like it was.

The truth, which we now know thanks to us being in the future, is that the New Deal *didn't* save anyone from the Great Depression. In fact, four million additional people lost their jobs during the beginning of FDR's presidency, and he at times seemed completely at sea, freezing, backpedaling, and struggling to come up with a solution. Really, America's entrance into World War II is likely what saved the nation; the increase in jobs and government spending that a war necessitates put Americans back to work.

We know that *now*. At the time, however, FDR told the nation that his New Deal had saved the day and everyone believed him, because that was simply Roosevelt's way. His legs never technically healed, but he used braces and canes to present the *illusion* of mobility, so hey, he might as well be walking. His New Deal didn't fix the economy, but because he *said* it did, he pumped Americans full of faith and hope. Roosevelt's will was more powerful than reality. He navigated us through World War II and was elected to an unprecedented fourth term. He needed to die in office; it was the only way Americans would stop voting for him. Hell, I *still* write him in every four years.

That's not helpful. Sorry. Here's what you need to know about FDR, the man described by Lyndon Johnson as "the only person I ever knew, anywhere, who was never afraid." After overcoming the illness that resulted in his paralysis, he reportedly said, "If you had spent two years in bed trying to wiggle your big toe, after that everything else would seem easy." That includes walking again, swimming, being more president than anyone else will ever be, and, presumably, fighting you.

That was also not helpful. I am so, so sorry.

★ ★ ★ ★ ★ ★

★ ★ ★ ★ ★ ★

IF YOU CAN'T TAKE

HARRY TRUMAN'S

HEAT, STOP GETTING PUNCHED BY HIM

★ ★ ★

Many of our presidents had tough or at least inspiring early lives. Lincoln was born in a log cabin and rose up to become president. Hoover cheated death. Grant was born in a barrel of whiskey and raised by snakes (I think, I'm not an expert).

Thirty-third president Harry S. Truman—not so much.

Unlike Jackson, who pursued fights as a child with the manic eagerness of someone who believed candy would fly out if he beat his enemies hard enough, Truman ran from fights. Literally. Schoolyard bullies often chose Truman as the target of their aggression, and he chose the "flight" option and bolted at the first sign of trouble. Truman preferred to spend his childhood reading or braiding his sister's hair. His only childhood injury of note was a broken collarbone, which he received when he accidentally knocked himself out of his chair *while combing his hair,* which is the most embarrassing way to break your collarbone that doesn't involve pooping yourself.

For a long time, Truman was very unremarkable. He spent many years trying to start businesses so he could have enough money to leave home (he lived on a farm that was *also* very unremarkable), but he failed, consistently. Business after business went under, sending Truman deeper and deeper into debt. It seemed, for the first twenty years or so of his life, Truman was as good at running a business as he was at not breaking his collarbone after brushing his precious hair too hard (which is to say, "not very").

Unfortunately for you, it looks like Truman got all of the cowardice and failure out of his system early, because all of that fight-fleeing, hair-braiding, and general pussifying in which Truman so regularly engaged stopped dead when he got older. It seems that decades of running from fights turned into a burning desire to get *into* fights when he was older, which might be why he signed up to fight in World War I back in 1917. Despite how bad he was at literally everything he'd ever tried, Truman advanced quickly in the military and, in 1918, was made captain of Battery D (also known as "Dizzy D"), a unit of 194 soldiers who were known for their drunkenness and rowdiness. This was a unit that many considered "uncommandable," and in fact Truman was made captain of their regiment only because they'd already driven the previous two captains away with their wild antics, refusal to listen to authority, and overall assholishness. Most assumed that Truman, with his limited fighting experience and his nerdy glasses, would quit before you could say "Hey, it's like the military version of *Dangerous Minds*!"

Surprisingly, in a few weeks, Truman turned the uncommandable unit of drunken-ass clowns into a well-disciplined and efficient fight squad. He spoke to them plainly and simply and in a language that they understood (which, in Battery D's case, meant a shitload of goddamn cursing. Bitch. Farts). Truman warned his troops that if any of them didn't think they could get along with him, he would punch them in the nose (because that would make them get along with him better?). On the subject of cursing, one of his troops said, "I never heard a man cuss so well or so intelligently . . . The battery didn't say a word. They must have figured the cap'n could do the cussin' for the whole outfit."

Just one month after Truman took command, the unit came under fire from its German enemies, and when the men panicked and tried to flee (running, as Truman so often had as a child, from the fight), Truman stood his ground and started yelling and cursing at them. He screamed and insulted and belittled anyone who tried to leave, and let rip a string of profanities. The men of Battery D were so moved by Truman's determination and filthy mouth that, one by one, they all came back and stood with him, all while still under enemy fire. This band of unruly jerks was prepared to stay and die for Truman, but they would never actually need to; Truman marched his unit all over France, taking out Germans every step along the way, and never lost a single man. Maybe if one of the German soldiers had handed Truman a comb, things would have been different, but, as things are, Truman left the war a hero.

Truman parlayed his status as a war hero into a job in politics, which is certainly a step down in terms of badassedness but a step up in not-getting-shot-at-ness. As a Missouri senator, he became well-known for his decency and honesty. Truman was a hard worker who spent his time cracking down on corruption in the government and, in particular, the military. He formed special committees that were put in place to make sure no money was being wasted and that none of the weapons, vehicles, and uniforms being used by America's soldiers were defective or shoddy.

He did *such* a good job that then-president FDR demanded that Truman be his vice president leading into his final term. At first it was a request, but when Truman seemed reluctant to take the job, it *became* a demand. As tough and as confident as he became in the war, Truman was still nervous at heart. Truman's first words on learning that FDR had hand-picked him specifically were "Oh, shit."

When FDR died, thrusting Truman into the presidential . . . throne? Hammock? I don't know where presidents sit. Beanbag chair, probably . . . Anyway, Truman stepped up. Truman is one of the few men tasked with filling in for one of the greatest presidents we've ever had, which is no easy feat. It was a tough act to follow, but Truman performed admirably.

Still, like most presidents, Truman had a sneaky, devious side too. He brought his honesty and integrity into the White House, but didn't hold on to it for long; he made tough choices when he felt like he needed to. Tough and, let's say, unpresidential and possibly illegal choices.

Put yourself in Truman's shoes; it's 1947, World War II is over, but you still want to keep a large military presence in Eastern Europe to keep the Soviets from taking over governments in various European countries like Hungary and Austria. Unfortunately, the American people don't *want* to devote the time/money/resources that such a thing would require, because Americans in 1947 didn't really give a crap about what happened to the government in Austria. But you're not the American people, you're President Truman. And you *want* that strong, powerful international presence. You want to go over to Europe and establish America as an international peace-maker/police force. So what do you do? You convince the country that they're a heartbeat away from another war.

You lie.

It's true that the Soviets in the 1940s weren't exactly the "good guys," but that doesn't change the fact that Truman manipulated information and had people outright lie for him to scare the ever-loving shit out of the American people. Truman had Lucius Clay, the commander of military forces in Europe (and a man who personally believed that American troops in Eastern Europe were "as secure . . . as they would be at home"), write a letter to Congress claiming he believed that war could break out at any minute. A *general* who wrote private letters talking about how secure everyone was, was ordered to *lie to Congress* to scare the American people enough to green-light whatever Truman wanted for this looming war.

The truth was that the Soviet Union was in no real shape to wage a war at the time; they simply weren't strong enough. But Truman wanted the draft reinstated and more money for the military, so he bent and broke the truth and warned everybody about a war that wasn't coming. (It worked, by the way.)

Truman may have made a name for himself in politics by seeking and taking out corruption in governmental committees, but he is one sneaky motherfucker. He's not one of the bigger or stronger presidents, but he's certainly one of the most devious, especially when he thinks he's right. Like Jackson, Truman has a fiery temper and isn't afraid to show it off—so much so that David Lilienthal, chairman of the Atomic Energy Commission, was generally afraid that Truman's tendency to occasionally flip out would bring about World War III. That's not hyperbole. Truman was the president who dropped the bomb. *This was a real concern*. Be on guard.

Also, one time he said that "being a president is like riding a tiger."

So Truman knows how to ride a tiger. Hopefully he won't bring one to your fight.

DWIGHT D. EISENHOWER

ONLY KNOWS HOW TO FIGHT
AND BE PRESIDENT

★ ★ ★

While we know now that most presidents were super crazy, there's a fairly clear pattern to the *kind* of craziness. Modern presidents were crazy *ambitious* and obsessed with power to an unhealthy degree, while early presidents were crazy in a more general, certifiable sort of way. A way that develops when you're born before laws and decency have been invented.

Dwight D. Eisenhower ("Ike"), our thirty-fourth president, bucked the trend of modern presidents and embraced a tradition of old-school aggressive insanity pioneered by men like Andrew Jackson and George Washington. He was an early-1800s kind of crazy in a 1960s world. Even his name was tough as shit (*Eisenhower* is German for "one who cuts iron"), meaning Ike was born several degrees more badass than you, right at birth.

Ike spent most of his childhood getting into fistfights and settling real or imagined scores with enemies using his tiny, bald fists. If he didn't have any schoolyard bullies to take on, Eisenhower would take on nature; once when he wasn't allowed out on Halloween, he punched a tree trunk until his knuckles bled. Rumor has it that, if you listen closely every October 31, you can still hear that tree crying, desperately trying to figure out what it had to do with Ike's Halloween.

When Ike grew up and ran out of trees to humiliate, he served in the army and excelled at it. While he never personally saw any action, he thrived as a commander, a man who had a high military IQ and knew how to plan attacks and inspire men to follow him. Ike was so good in the military that he never really tried to do anything else. In between World Wars I and II, Eisenhower stuck around in the general field of warfare, even though there were no wars to fight. He studied military history and worked on and wrote about tanks. It's very likely, in fact, that Ike's decision to build the Interstate Highway System as president was based on his time working on tanks; he didn't think the tanks were traveling across the country fast enough for his tastes, so he *built an entire highway system*. He earned so many different badass military titles, some of which (Military Governor, Supreme Allied Commander), sound completely made up, and he even taught himself to fly a plane (even though no one asked him to), just in case he ever wanted to dabble in being a fighter pilot at some point. Ike was just a professional soldier, running tanks and killing bad guys for his nine-to-five.

As Captain Doctor Supreme Allied Commander Wizard of Military Forces during World War II, Eisenhower orchestrated the Allied invasion of Normandy, made famous by *Saving Private Ryan* and one of the better *Medal of Honor* video games. Eisenhower originally scheduled the invasion for June 5, because the tides were in Allied favor (there were only ten days in any given month when the tides *would* be favorable to an invasion of this kind), but he had to delay it as a result of bad weather that would have resulted in the loss of who *knows* how many troops. The weather was *also* supposed to be terrible on June 6, but Ike was tired of letting God delay his plans and so he ordered the invasion. Even though a huge storm was *supposed* to hit, it didn't, and the weather cleared up at the last minute. Was it simply luck, or did nature, as a result of Eisenhower's established reputation as a bloodthirsty tree-boxer, retreat out of fear of Ike's wrath? It is the perhaps obvious stance of this book that luck had nothing to do with it; God had seen what Ike was capable of and would not dare cross him.

The Invasion of Normandy was a major turning point in the war and allowed Ike to add Super Sexy Supreme Defeater of Adolf Hitler to his already impressive military résumé.

When America ran out of made-up military titles to give Ike, they made him president. One of Ike's first orders of business involved looking at the Korean War—a complex, lengthy, and involved struggle—and saying, "Yeah, that's enough of that," and ending the hell out of it with a single swing of his massive balls. As much as Ike loved war, and as skilled as he was as a military strategist, he wasn't going to let his own passions dictate how he would run the country. Eisenhower ended the Korean War during his presidency and did so without involving America in any other wars, because he wanted peace and believed it could be achieved. When the Department of Defense demanded more money for more bombs, Ike turned them down, asking, "How many times do we need to destroy Russia?" When Senator Joseph McCarthy went on the wild Communist witch hunt that divided America, Eisenhower worked behind the scenes to get McCarthy censured (the political version of "Shut the fuck up"). Eisenhower worked behind the scenes on that, by the way, because, in his words, he "refused to get in a pissing contest with a skunk," because presidents talked cooler back then than they do today. America didn't "lose a soldier or a foot of ground" during Ike's administration. President Eisenhower controlled the arms race and kept the peace.

Still, don't let Ike's peacekeeping and the fact that he never personally served on the frontlines in any battle fool you into thinking our most tree-fightingest president wasn't tough. By the time Ike was halfway through his presidency, he'd had a screwed-up knee, malaria, tuberculosis, high blood pressure, spinal malformation, shingles, neuritis, one heart attack, one stroke, Crohn's disease, and bronchitis. That's all according to his official medical history, but if you'd asked Eisenhower or read his diary at the time, you'd see that *he* casually summed up the whole ordeal by saying "lots of troubles with my insides lately." That's it. Not "Boy, it sure feels like death inside my body, all of the time, holy shit." Just "lots of troubles . . . *lately.*"

It took six heart attacks to eventually kill Ike, and it's still not clear if the heart attacks did it or Eisenhower simply willed himself to death. On what would turn out to be his deathbed, his last words were "I want to go; God take me." The message was clear: wars, diseases, and heart attacks don't stop Eisenhower; *he* decides when he's good and goddamn ready to die, and then you'd better do as he says.

Make sure you work that weak knee; he injured it playing football in college and it's never been the same since. He is without a doubt a better strategist than you are and has likely looked at your fight from three or four different angles, as he did every problem, but a lifetime of *planning* battles doesn't mean he'll be prepared to defend himself in a street fight to the death. Anyone can sit in an office and say "Now go kill Hitler," but it takes a different person entirely to walk up to a president and kick him in the nuts. I want you to *be that kind of person.*

JOHN F. KENNEDY

WILL KNOCK YOUR ASS

BACK, AND TO THE LEFT

★ ★ ★

From 1961 until 1963, the United States of America was a high school football team, and John F. Kennedy was the dreamy quarterback that we all respected and lusted after. Plenty of presidents have been as good as Kennedy, and many have been *better*, but he is the only president that made the American people, in unison, say, "What a cool dude. I'd let him have sex with my girlfriend, if she was into it."

The Kennedy chapter shouldn't be entirely about boning, but it should be *mostly* about boning, so let's start by talking about how good Kennedy was at boning: Very. Or, if not very, then *thoroughly.* Kennedy admitted to friends and visiting diplomats that he wouldn't be satisfied if he didn't have sex at least three times every day, and he once told the prime minister of the United Kingdom that, if he went more than three days without at least one woman, he'd get terrible headaches. Kennedy talked about having threesomes with the kind of casual dismissal that we normal folks reserve for talking about getting gas before work. "Gas prices sure are getting high," we'll say. "Having sex with two women at the same time is a neat thing that I do very often," Kennedy would reply.

Kennedy's list of sexual exploits include Marilyn Monroe, Jayne Mansfield, Angie Dickinson, Brazilian actress Florinda Bolkan, and, if you happen to have a grandmother who was an intern during Kennedy's presidency then, sorry, but your grandma. In all statistical likelihood, John F. Kennedy had sex with your grandmother. It's nothing personal, he was just a handsome robot that needed vagina to fuel his engines, and that's okay, because his engines were running the country.

According to interviews with some of the many, many interns Kennedy slept with during his presidency, there was no passion or emotional connection in sex for Kennedy; he simply wanted to do it, nap, do it again, nap, do it again, nap, be president, do it again, and on and on until there were no more women left for him to sleep with. As a matter of fact, the only times that Kennedy actually *did* get emotional came, according to his sister, "when he loses." Kennedy's father, Joseph Kennedy, taught his sons the "Kennedy standards," which referred not to helping people or leading a good life, but to *winning.* Kennedy boys were told not to play a sport "unless [they] could be captain," and that "second place was a failure." Little Jack would respond, a few decades later, by becoming captain of both fucking and America.

JFK was our most James Bondian president, and not just because he had an impossible amount of sex that he approached with the haunting detachment of a sociopath; he also had a proven track record of badassedry to boot. Kennedy had a back injury that disqualified him from serving in the army, but instead of just seizing the opportunity to avoid getting shot at by bad guys without looking like a coward, he used his influential father's connections to sneak his way into the navy. That's right. While most overprivileged kids use their rich daddies to get out of speeding tickets or get into good colleges, Kennedy begged *his* father for a favor that would result in people trying to *shoot and kill him,* because Kennedy is a breed of real-life action hero we simply stopped making.

In August of 1943, Kennedy's boat (the *PT-109*) was ripped in two by the Japanese destroyer *Amagiri*. The boat was unsalvageable, the crew was disoriented, and there were flames everywhere, but Kennedy, even on his worst day, could not be flapped. He addressed his crew and asked if they wanted to fight or surrender. "There's nothing in the book about a situation like this," Kennedy said. "What do you want to do? *I have nothing to lose.*" (Sidebar: whoever made the Hollywood movie based on the attacks on Kennedy's boat and crew should be shot for titling it *PT 109* instead of *Nothing to Lose.* Come on, Hollywood.)

Kennedy, despite that chronic back injury and a newly ruptured spinal disc, swam four hours to an island with his crew. If you're not impressed by that, you should know that he did it while towing an injured crewman by the life-jacket strap. And if you're not impressed by that, you should know that he did the towing with his *teeth*. And if you're not impressed by that, you should know that when they realized there was no food on the island, they swam to a *new* island, with Kennedy *again* towing an injured crewman with his teeth. And if you're not impressed by that, *bullshit,* of course you are.

In your fight with Kennedy, try not to have sex with him, as it will only make him stronger. Second of all, despite all of the badass things written about Kennedy in books, including and especially this one, he was actually a much weaker man than most people knew. Kennedy acted the part of a healthy, young, virile man of power, partly because he never wanted to dwell on or grant credence to any of his illnesses, and partly to inspire the American people with a leader they could really get behind (and vice versa, *if you know what Kennedy's sayin'*). He was plagued by various illnesses (including Addison's disease), and was born with the left side of his body smaller than the right, which is where all of his back problems came from. Kennedy's back was so bad that he wore a metal back brace and, when he was out of view of the press, would often use crutches or even a wheelchair to get around. The truth is that Kennedy was

sick and in pain his entire life; he just refused to accept it because he didn't want it to hold him back (and because "Kennedy boys don't cry" was another one of the infamous "Kennedy standards"). He was in denial. He presented an image of vitality, but make no mistake: Kennedy was always hurting.

Still, he's going to try to use his injuries and poor health to his advantage just as much as you will. Constantly sick and accident-prone as a child, Kennedy thrived on the idea that death was constantly around the corner, waiting for him. He'd had so many surgeries, so many life-threatening illnesses—he was on what many believed to be his deathbed no less than *three separate times* in his life—that he lived every day like it might be his last. His personal secretary said that he tried "to crowd as much living as possible into every single hour." *That's* why he told his crew he had "nothing to lose" and was prepared to go into battle even after his boat was torn right in half, and that's why he drove himself to become the youngest president in his lifetime. Hell, it's arguable that he accomplished as much as he did in his brief presidency because the specter of premature death loomed over his shoulder at every waking minute.

So, you know, work the back and all, but prepare for a long, bitter, and stubborn fight. "Expect death at every turn" and "Second place is a failure" are the two principles that guided Kennedy through everything he did in life.

Also: "I fuck for fuel." That was another one of his principles. Probably less relevant to his fight with you, but it's important to point out, all the same.

LYNDON JOHNSON:

★ ★ ★

Pull just about any president out of a hat and you'll hear the same story: "I had no ambition to be the president of the United States, but God ['the people'] seemed to *want* me to be president; I humbly accept God's plan and I am hereby announcing my candidacy for the presidency." Washington created the mold by being the farmer who reluctantly became a soldier who reluctantly became a commander who reluctantly became the politician, and every president since has followed in his faux-humble footsteps.

Except Lyndon Johnson.

Johnson always wanted to be the president. In *grade school* Johnson was telling his classmates that he was going to be the president one day, and as he grew up he never stopped saying "I want to be the president." He just altered it and started saying, "I want to be *the best* president." It takes an impossibly giant ego to look at the office of the presidency, in all of its enormities and with all of its responsibilities, and think, "I could do that." Johnson looked at his heroes like FDR and thought, "I could do that *better.*"

This was because LBJ is the only president who was acutely aware of how *fucking cool* it was to be president. He knew that it was an important job, and one to be taken seriously, and yada yada yada, but he also knew that it was pretty damn badass. Johnson was addressing some troops in Vietnam and, after his speech, right when he was about to make his exit in a military helicopter, one of the members of his staff asked which helicopter was his and he replied, "Son, *all* these helicopters are mine." Those are the words of a man who thinks he's above the law, the words of a man who knows he's entitled to one "freebie kill" as president and isn't afraid to use it on you.

It wasn't *just* the coolness that attracted Johnson; mostly, it was the power, and to Johnson, power was *everything.*

Everything Johnson did as president was about demonstrating this power. Whenever he wanted something from a senator or visiting diplomat, he would employ what came to be known as the "Johnson Treatment." Utilizing his impressive 6'3" frame, Johnson would get in someone's face and *loom*, right over them, looking down at them and presenting a physical reminder that his literal and figurative status dwarfed theirs. He would badger and yell and spit and mock, all while being just a few inches away from someone's face. It was about intimidation; everyone was powerless against the Johnson Treatment.

If towering over someone wasn't demeaning enough, he'd also make people watch him poop. If you needed to go over important business with the president, he'd listen for a bit and, every once in a while, have you follow him into the bathroom and plead your case while he nonchalantly pooped. If there's a more efficient demonstration of power, I've certainly never heard it (unless, of course, the president ever thought to combine the Johnson Treatment with the ol' Watch Me Poop technique).

There's even an old White House legend that says LBJ once peed on a member of the Secret Service. On. *On!* According to the rumors, Johnson was standing next to an agent at some function

when he noticed that he was mostly blocked from the public view. So, using the Secret Service agent as both shield and urinal, he pulled out his . . . johnson, and started peeing, right on the agent's leg. The agent protested and Johnson said, "That's all right, son. It's my prerogative." And how could you argue with that? If anyone is legally allowed to pee on another person, it would have to be the president.

Finally, it would be irresponsible of me as a student of both History and Doing It to not bring up the pimping.

My God, the pimping.

Like Kennedy before him, Johnson saw the presidency as a noble and sacred calling that would render pimping easy (despite the fact that the field was widely believed by most leading pimp scientists to be decidedly "not easy"). Johnson liked having sex, was proud of the amount he'd had, and would get furious when White House staffers would talk about Kennedy's near-legendary skills as a cocksman. He would often say that he'd bed "more women accidentally than Kennedy ever did on purpose." It's unclear how exactly one would accidentally have sex with multiple women, but if Johnson says he did it, then he did.

Johnson could often be found hitting on other women right in front of his wife, and if you think *that's* the most outrageous display of his sexual appetite, you haven't read the next sentence yet. Lyndon Johnson, as president, would take his dick out and shake it at people. Sometimes he was trying to impress people, and sometimes he would do it if one of his staffers dared challenge him. He'd be confronted with a problem and then out came the dick (he called it "Jumbo," because when you're the president, that's the kind of thing you're allowed to do). Before you could say "Hey, put that away, we're in the middle of a staff meeting and yes I regret using the word 'staff,'" he would wave Jumbo around and ask you if you'd "ever seen anything as big as this?" (That'll probably happen when he fights you.) According to biographer Robert Dallek, at one point during his presidency, Johnson met with a reporter who repeatedly asked him why American troops were in Vietnam. Frustrated, Johnson unzipped his pants, pulled out his "substantial organ," and shouted, "This is why!" The craziest part of this story, which itself is nothing but pure, poop-eating crazy, is that it *worked*. That answer *satisfied* the reporter, like "Oh, yeah, when you put it that way, *sure*. Of *course* we're in Vietnam—look at that dick. We should be in *all countries*. I'd be starting a war on Space if I had a dick like yours. Come on, now."

Still, it wasn't all poop shows and dick waving in the Johnson administration. This chapter is called "Johnson: The Puppet Master" because Johnson knew how to take control. He took control of the presidency after the shocking death of JFK, and he took control of all of his opponents. He kept dossiers on every single person in the Senate. He knew what they wanted, knew what they liked, and he knew their weaknesses. One biography states that he would "get up every day and learn what their fears, their desires, their wishes, their wants were and he could then manipulate, dominate, persuade and cajole them." If he was dealing with a particularly short senator, he'd grab them by the lapels and lift them straight into the air. He was like a big, presidential bully, cornering members of the Senate and leaning over them while they backpedaled helplessly, badgering them until they submitted to his demands. "Stop hitting yourself," he probably said to one or two uppity senators, whilst whipping them with his own penis.

If Jackson's presidential cocktail was heavy on the passion, and Arthur's was heavy on the ambition, then Johnson's was heavy on the ego, and *that's* going to be the key to winning this fight. He's not just going to want to beat you, he's going to want to *dominate* you and show off in some kind of primal display of alpha male strength. Never give him the satisfaction on which he thrives. When he looms over you, spit right in his face. When he tries to make you watch him poop, say, "No *thank you*." When he pulls out his dick, *laugh at it* and say, "Boy, that's the sorriest piece of presidential genitalia since Grant." Sure, this will make him very mad (and he *was* a big athletic guy), but it will also make him *sloppy*. Get in his head by repeatedly reminding him that he's not the greatest president of all time (he'll *hate* that), and you just might have a shot.

RICHARD NIXON:

THE SWEATIEST THING TO PUNCH

ANOTHER THING SINCE GEORGE FOREMAN

BOXED A GRIZZLY BEAR IN A SAUNA

★ ★ ★

Richard His-Mom's-Maiden-Name Nixon will forever go down as one of the worst presidents of all time, and that is a fact. History will never vindicate his actions. He'll be associated with sliminess and an inflated sense of jowly entitlement for the rest of human existence. His pathetic slovenliness and hilarious sweatiness in the first televised debates are the reasons every presidential campaign today has a budget for a wardrobe and makeup specialist.

His hideousness invented a job.

Before all that, Nixon was practically born to be horrible. He was sick his entire life and never well liked, and psychoanalysts who have looked into Nixon have described him as "lonely, hypersensitive, narcissistic, suspicious and secretive," and a man who "lied to gain love, to shore up his grandiose fantasies, to bolster his ever-wavering sense of identity. He lied in attack, hoping to win." The fact that we made him president is one of the most frightening things in history, but we can rest assured that *he* made that happen, and that sin wasn't on us (more on this later!).

Nixon had two nicknames his whole life: "Gloomy Gus" (given to him in college, because of his constant seriousness) and "Tricky Dick" (as president, because of his trickiness, and the fact that he was a dick). Three, if you count "Slimeballs McShithead," the nickname that this book coined for him, just now (because he left a trail of sweat-slime in his wake, and because "McShithead" is a funny word). He served in the navy but saw no actual combat, hated sports, never exercised, and was once called a "no-good lying bastard" by Harry Truman. Every fact in this paragraph is unrelated; I just wanted to Rolodex a bunch of awful Nixon things.

One of the most unfortunate things about Nixon from a critical perspective is that he *did* do a few good things while in office. He extended America's reach all the way to the moon, and even though we can't do anything with it and never hang out there, it's important to know that it's ours and no one else is allowed to touch it. Nixon got us out of Vietnam and was the first American president to visit China. There. I promised the publisher I'd spend at least a hundred words saying vaguely nice things about Nixon, just to make sure the book doesn't come off as too biased, and now that I've done that, we can move on to our regularly scheduled programming.

Did you know that President McShithead plotted to kill someone while in office? True story. It wasn't a horrible dictator he plotted to kill, like a good president would, but a *journalist,* like a horrible dictator would. Jack Anderson was an okay journalist who chased Nixon throughout his entire career. Anderson believed Nixon was corrupt and dedicated his life to exposing that corruption, and it drove Nixon *crazy,* because Anderson was pesky and manipulative, and *totally right.* Several confidential tapes reveal Nixon and his attorney general obsessing over Anderson, and figuring out if they were going to discredit him or kill him (John Mitchell wanted to hang Anderson, which prompted Nixon to say, "Goddamn it, yes . . . we've got to do something with this son of a bitch"). Nixon and his team also

contemplated murdering Anderson by either hiding poison in his medicine cabinet or smearing a lethal dose of LSD on his steering wheel. Two things: 1) Nixon, please, *stop taping your freaking schemes, you idiot*; and 2) "Lethal dose"? You think you can kill someone with LSD? Man, you never even *tried* to understand the hippies, Nixon.

If plotting to kill and discredit one person isn't devious enough for you, Nixon also had no problem ruining the whole world. In the 1968 election, his opponent, Hubert Humphrey (Johnson's vice president), was pulling ahead in the polls because he singlehandedly made great strides toward peace in Vietnam leading up to the election. He called for a bombing halt and Vietnam *agreed*. America and North Vietnam were just a few days away from total peace, and the American people were a few days away from electing their next president, but Nixon was born in slime, so none of that mattered to him. The day before the election, Nixon sabotaged the peace talks by convincing America's allies in South Vietnam to back out, warning them that they were going to get "sold out" if they went ahead with this whole peace thing. Without the momentum of the peace talks behind Humphrey, he lost the election to Richard Nixon, who publicly criticized Humphrey for his inability to deliver.

Just to make sure this lands, here it is again: Nixon extended the war in Vietnam by five years just so he could screw Humphrey out of the White House and become president, where he could be shitty on a much grander scale.

But, hey, maybe Richard Nixon had a *better* strategy to end the war. Maybe he had his own plans for how to end the war and wanted to implement them as president. Maybe it was even more peaceful, right?

Well, he did have his own strategy, but if you know your history or how cheap rhetorical devices work, you already know that Nixon's plan *wasn't* more peaceful than Humphrey's. Nixon favored what he called the "Madman Theory," but what is commonly known among Pop Culture enthusiasts like you and me as the "Good Cop/ Bad Cop Routine." Nixon wanted to convince the North Vietnamese that he was *crazy* and could snap at any minute. Nixon legitimately said to his advisors, "We'll just slip them the word that, 'for God's sake, you know Nixon is obsessed about Communism. We can't constrain him when he's angry—and he has his hand on the nuclear button.'" Nixon *said that shit.* It would have been pretty badass, but the problem is that every Bad Cop needs a Good Cop, and Nixon didn't have one, because there's only one president. So there was no Good Cop being reasonable and calming down the Bad Cop; there was just the Bad Cop who, in his own words, wanted to "bomb the bastards off the earth," and *damn near tried.* In 1972, he bombed for twelve straight days. No one bombs for twelve days *strategically;* that is the move of a literal, clinical, certifiable lunatic.

Eventually, Nixon did effectively end U.S. involvement in the Vietnam War. Not thanks to the Madman Theory, obviously, that's idiotic, but because Nixon agreed to remove all troops from the war and spend some time and money rebuilding North Vietnam, as long as American prisoners of war were returned. Call it "retreating" or "very expensive retreating," if you want to split hairs, but Nixon did get our troops home. Got them home from a war that *could* have ended already if he hadn't extended it five years for his own political gain because he sucks, but he still got them home, nonetheless. Yay, Nixon.

The House Judiciary Committee famously voted to impeach Nixon for obstruction of justice and abuse of power, and he resigned the presidency after one of his many horrible, slimy scandals caught up with him, and, much to the chagrin of everyone, was given a full pardon by his successor, Gerald Ford. He was never indicted for any of the horrible things he did, only a *fraction* of which are covered in this chapter, and he spent the rest of his life dismissing the crimes as simple "blunders."

Richard Nixon is one of the most dangerous men in this book. He's not fighting for redemption; that's out of the question. He has no image to protect, no legacy to preserve, and, since the nation has already collectively turned its back, nothing to prove to anyone. The only person Nixon will be fighting for is Nixon. He has nothing to lose. He is fearless, unpredictable, impossibly slippery, and has absolutely no soul. It'll be like boxing Evil incarnate (but right after Evil showered and refused to towel off. President Nixon was very sweaty, and that's funny and gross to me. Was that not clear?).

GERALD FORD

CAN'T FIGHT YOU UNTIL HE FINISHES

HIS BATTLE WITH GRAVITY

★ ★ ★

It's unfortunate that Gerald "His Actual First Name was Leslie and We Should Really Be Making Fun of Him for That More Often" Ford will historically only be remembered for one of two things: his pardoning of Nixon and his inexplicable tendency to fall down with shocking regularity. Few people know just how *tough* Ford was (given that he spent nineteen hours of any given day already in mid-fall, he'd sort of have to be). Ford was an athlete his whole life, excelling at football through high school and college. His coaches often marveled at how sharp and meticulous he was, saying that having Ford on a team was like having an extra coach on the field. Ford's high football IQ, attention to detail, athleticism, and shockingly high threshold for taking blows to the head were so impressive that he was offered huge salaries by both the Detroit Lions and Green Bay Packers to play professional football, but he turned them down and decided to focus on law. He didn't have enough money for law school but got accepted to Yale, on the condition that he coach Yale's undergraduate boxing program (he accepted).

That's only really striking when you realize that Ford had never boxed in his entire life. Yale took him on face value alone and said, "Your grades aren't *quite* good enough for law school, but we'll let that slide because you look like a man who could train people how to beat the shit out of other people," and Ford simply responded, "Sounds about right." Because he didn't make enough money as a boxing coach, he spent his summers working as a professional bear-feeder, which is a title I would *pretend* to hold to impress women if it didn't sound so completely made up. But it's true. Ford was a park ranger/bear-feeder at Yellowstone National Park, because someone needed to feed the bears and that fell under the category of tough-guy things that Ford assumed he'd rule at. He also, randomly, worked briefly as a male model and appeared on the cover of the April 1942 issue of *Cosmopolitan*. He's a dumb guy with a bunch of random jobs under his belt who ended up spending a ton of time in the White House; basically, Gerald Ford's life story is like a less believable *Forrest Gump*.

After Pearl Harbor, Ford put his law degree on hold and hung up his boxing gloves and, I don't know, bear-feeding nunchucks and male-model underpants, so he could pursue killing all of the bad guys who hated America. He joined the navy and quickly rose from ensign to lieutenant commander. He was then made a naval fitness instructor (teaching big, tough navy men how to be bigger, tougher, navier men). This might have been enough action for your average guy, but Ford was raised in the school of hard knocks (Yale, I guess?) and he wanted *more*, so he requested a transfer to the USS *Monterey*, a light-aircraft carrier that appeared in almost every major battle in the South Pacific. As if that wasn't enough, God decided to join the war and sent massive typhoons to attack the *Monterey* and three American destroyers. The other three ships capsized and lost most of their crews, and Ford's ship almost tipped over and burst into flames. As the ship tipped twenty-five degrees to one side, Ford lost his footing on the deck and started sliding toward the ocean and

would have fallen right in if he hadn't caught hold of the rim of the deck *with his foot*. He readjusted, got himself to a safe place on the boat, and put out the fire (later admitting that he "never had any fear of death during the war," which, when your boat is sideways and on fire, is *literally impossible*).

Ford never went to hide below deck or anything, he just stood up top in the storm, watching his ship sway and burn, thinking, "Nope. Still not fearing death." By the time he left the war, Ford had accumulated ten battle stars. A man who has enough battle stars that he can comfortably throw a few of them at you like ninja shurikens and still have a bunch left over to intimidate bears is *not* a man to be fucked with, no matter how many fashion runways he walks down.

After the war, Ford was bitten by the politics bug and made a name for himself (not Leslie; a different name), as a hardworking, honest politician of integrity. He never lied, never told a half-truth, never manipulated anyone, and never did anything that he didn't think was right. His moral streak earned the admiration of Republicans and Democrats alike. His Homer Simpson–esque plainspoken nature mixed well with his Homer Simpson–esque appearance and, when he succeeded Nixon and promised to restore integrity and honesty to the White House, America was ready to believe him.

And then he pardoned Nixon and America was like, "Oh, blow me, you clumsy fart."

The hard truth was that pardoning Nixon was the right thing to do. Sure, declaring that everything a person had done over a five-year period was fine and legal without ever even knowing what Nixon had done is kind of a boner, but at the time, Ford needed to close the book on the whole Nixon thing if he wanted to get anything done. He saw a country with a failing economy and a military that was second-best in a time when second-best wasn't an option, but all anyone wanted to talk about was "Nixon this and Nixon that." So Ford made the tough call and granted Nixon an absolute pardon, because it was a more official way of ending the conversation than saying "Just shut the fuck up and let me be president already."

It was a tough call that wasn't going to earn Ford any friends (except Nixon, which, *gross*), but making tough calls was Ford all over. Unfortunately, Ford's decision to unconditionally pardon Nixon without even hearing what his crimes were ruined the reputation of honesty and openness he'd spent his life building (and it would eventually be the single issue that cost him reelection). Despite his integrity and impressive naval career, *that's* what folks remember about Ford: pardoning Nixon.

That and the falling, *Lord*, the falling. Part of Ford's reputation as a klutz was brought on by a media that turned on him post-pardon, but an even larger part of it was based on Ford being a klutz. He looked dumb, spoke slowly and awkwardly, he tripped getting out of Air Force One, and once while golfing hit a random person with his ball directly in the head (and also again while playing tennis). And while boarding a train after a campaign speech in Michigan, he bumped his head because he missed the door.

Know that, going into your fight, Ford has probably already thonked himself in the dome like a dozen times en route to the ring. Also remember, however, his time as a star football player and his athletic prowess. Your best bet is to make him think you're an easy opponent. Ford's old football coaches agreed that Ford thrived in the hard games and only made mistakes in easy ones. Let him think he has the upper hand and, when he least expects it, bash him on the head and give him his third concussion of the afternoon.

If all else fails, remind him that his real name is Leslie and he used to be a male model, and then laugh at him. Laugh and laugh.

RONALD REAGAN

IS LIKE A JOHN WAYNE
AND WOLVERINE HYBRID

★ ★ ★

Viral pneumonia, diverticulosis, a cancerous colon tumor, and a close-range bullet all have one thing in common: none of them had anything to do with Ronald Reagan's death, despite the fact that they were all present in his life. In fact, even though he's the oldest man to ever hold the office of president, Reagan was also one of the fittest, and being one of the most fit on a list that includes people who juggle Indian clubs and have duels and are Roosevelts is pretty damn impressive. Being strong is one thing, but Reagan displayed a unique ability to survive the kinds of things that would crush most men. It would be mildly irresponsible to suggest a definite relationship between President Ronald Reagan and fictional superhero Wolverine (who was known for his toughness, accelerated healing ability, and metal bones), but it would be morally reprehensible to not even *mention* the similarities. I'll just occasionally pepper in a few of the parallels in a historically responsible fashion and invite you, the reader, to draw your own conclusions.

Ronald Reagan's focus on fitness and athleticism started early; as a teenager, he worked as a lifeguard, a job that, for some reason, involved waking up every day and chopping a three-hundred-pound block of ice down into a one-hundred-pound block of ice. It's not clear *why* the particular camp where Reagan worked as a lifeguard required him to do that, but he did it seven days a week and, like Lincoln before him, used the repeated chopping motion to strengthen his arms. During his tenure as a lifeguard, Reagan managed to save seventy-seven lives, including one guy who Reagan rescued after another lifeguard *had already given up on the man*.

Saving lives, while undeniably Wolverine-esque, isn't necessarily *specific* to Wolverine, as plenty of people save lives, so let's get into that previously mentioned bullet, because that's one of Reagan's more Wolveriney stories. On March 30, 1981, Reagan visited the famous Ford's Theatre in Washington, DC. He looked at the presidential box where Lincoln was shot and idly thought about how easily *he* could also be shot, even with all of the protection with which modern presidents walked around. He pushed this morbid thought out of his head, shook it off, and then he got shot a few minutes later. A crazy man named John Hinckley Jr. fired six shots at President Reagan on the assumption that doing so would impress actress Jodie Foster (as of this writing, it still has not). One of those bullets hit Reagan's press secretary, one hit a Secret Service agent, one hit a local cop, two missed, and one hit Reagan, bouncing off of his seventh rib, puncturing and collapsing a lung, and landing one inch from his heart. (This seems as good a time as any to reiterate that the exploding bullet *bounced* off of Reagan's rib, almost as if his rib bone was *too strong* to be punctured, as if it was *made of adamantium, the strongest metal known to man*. While X-rays and medical professionals have never confirmed or even suggested that the former president's bones were made of adamantium, I, as a historian, am more responsible than science, so I will not callously rule it out as a possibility.) Reagan was then shoved roughly into the presidential limousine by a Secret Service agent but didn't even realize he'd been shot until he started coughing up blood a few seconds later. On the way to the hospital, Reagan lost three pints of blood.

Ronald Reagan wasn't like most men. When *Reagan* got to the hospital, there wasn't a stretcher or wheelchair waiting (sidebar: what a bullshit hospital), so he calmly stepped out of the car and casually walked himself into the emergency room without a problem. If you get a toy race car dislodged from your nose, they make you travel around in a wheelchair in the hospital, but Reagan, carrying on an apparent tradition of presidents who like walking around after getting shot, gets to stroll in with a bullet batting around an inch from his damn heart. Reagan didn't mention the bullet to the doctors, he just complained about experiencing a difficulty breathing, which we can go ahead and file under Most Misleading Understatement Ever.

Reagan's wife, Nancy, met him at the hospital and asked what

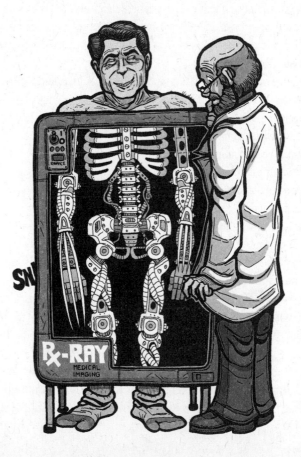

had happened, to which Reagan simply replied, "I forgot to duck." He did this—smile and crack jokes—throughout his entire stay at the hospital, exactly like a guy who *hadn't* just been shot (or like a guy who, for argument's sake, knew that the quick recovery time afforded to him by his superhuman accelerated-healing process would have him out of the hospital in no time). He even interrupted his own surgery to occasionally remove his oxygen mask and joke with the surgeons, saying "I hope you're a Republican," *after he'd lost half of his blood and they were cutting open his body to remove bullets.* Instead of resting after his successful surgery, Reagan stayed up all night entertaining the nurses with more jokes and anecdotes. Most seventy-year-olds would have died, but, according to his doctors, Reagan had the "physique of a thirty-year-old muscle builder" (which, incidentally, could also be said of hit Marvel character Wolverine, should anyone out there be considering continuing comparisons between these two iconic figures).

Twelve days after he'd been shot, President Ronald Reagan went back to work. Not only that, but he used the sympathy and support his injury brought him to push the bulk of his legislation through Congress, legislation that, had he not been playing the sympathy card, would never have made it out. Not only *that,* but he had a gym installed in the White House and gained so much muscle that he had to buy new suits. This was *after* he'd been shot. The man was seventy years old.

Reagan's toughness, his jokes, and his easygoing nature made him one of the most relatable presidents among Americans (he carried forty-nine out of fifty states in his second election), though many of his peers and certainly leaders abroad thought the actor-turned-cowboy-president was a lot of style and very little substance. Reagan was an effective communicator, unless he was mentioning facts or statistics, which he often got wrong, inspiring idiots who believed thinking with your *gut* was more important than thinking with your brain or the assistance of facts for decades to come. Even his critics abroad, however, couldn't pretend that Reagan wasn't a major factor in ending the Cold War. In one of the most shining displays of presidential badassery, Reagan thrilled the nation in 1987 when he went to Berlin, demanded an audience with the Soviet leader, and famously yelled, "Mr. Gorbachev, *suck my dick!*" Minutes later, the Berlin Wall fell, and with it, American fears of aggression from the Soviet Union.

(Real quick: one of Wolverine's archenemies, Omega Red, was *also* a communist. Two guys. Both hated communism. That's all.)

Reagan didn't see any action in his military career (he mostly worked on propaganda films), and didn't get in a lot of fights growing up, but his time spent on the football field—and the metal skeleton he may or may not have—has certainly toughened him up. I'd warn you that Reagan could probably take a good punch or two, but if you've read this far then you already know that the man can take a *bullet,* and I don't want to sit here and beat a dead horse or hit you over the head with something I've already told you.

Ronald Reagan is Wolverine. Ronald Reagan is Wolverine. Ronald Reagan is Wolverine.

BONUS CHAPTER:

ZOMBIE THEODORE ROOSEVELT

★ ★ ★

t Roosevelt's death, a fellow politician said, "Death had to take him sleeping, for if Roosevelt had been awake there would have been a fight." This historicomical book doesn't go so far as to presuppose that there *was* a fight and that, in fact, Death lost, but it also refuses to stoop to such levels of historical irresponsibility as to suggest that such a thing is *impossible*. In the interest of erring on the side of caution, this chapter will prepare you in case Roosevelt decides to a) not be dead, b) feast on human brains for sustenance, and c) track you down for pissing him off. Almost everything about the (living) Roosevelt chapter (and in particular the bits about you being physically, spiritually, and intellectually incapable of beating him), still apply, but there's an added level of impossibility: How do you kill a Theodore Roosevelt *that's already dead?!*

Well, let's start at the beginning and try to figure out *how* Theodore Roosevelt got infected with zombiism. The most likely scenario, insofar as any theory involving a fictional horror staple and a dead president can be "likely," is that he played with dead things too much. When he was just eight years old, Theodore Roosevelt was walking home when he came across the body of a dead seal in a New York marketplace. According to him, the corpse immediately filled him with "every possible feeling of romance and adventure." He would return to measure the corpse, and tried to find out how it died, and eventually took the skull home and kept it. TR built up his personal collection throughout his life, occasionally writing to his sister to brag about all of the dead birds and mice he had in his bedroom. If a non-bite-related way to catch "being a zombie" exists, it is my professional opinion that playing with skulls and growing up in a bedroom full of death is probably it.

So we'll assume that surrounding himself with corpses and obsessively embracing life is what brought TR to his current Presidential Zombie status. If standard zombie rules apply (and let's say they do), then the game hasn't changed; just remove the head and destroy the brain. Now, if standard Roosevelt rules apply (let's *obviously* say they do), then it won't be as simple as all that. TR was always prepared for everything. He's going to assume you know the whole "destroy the brain" thing and will likely try to gain an advantage. An advantage, in this case, means putting his head as far from your reach as possible. If you've been following closely, you already know what I'm about to say.

Theodore Roosevelt killed an elephant while on safari, gave it the zombie virus, and now he's riding a zombie elephant, right to your door.

Or a rhino. Roosevelt killed both in his days on safari, so there's really no telling what you're going to be facing (though, yes, it'll probably be one of those things). You're at a severe disadvantage, not just because TR's got the higher ground, but because he's the one who knows how to take down big game better than any other president (he and his son Kermit killed 11 elephants, 20 rhinos, and 17 lions); he'll know their weaknesses, so he'll know how to protect them against you.

The dangerous thing about zombies—the reason we all fear

them—comes from their numbers. A single zombie isn't intimidating; zombies are slow, awkward, and uncoordinated, and really only pose a threat when they've got an army. Roosevelt is a loner. Sure, he may have a rhino or lion or two, but he won't have raised a zombie army, because that takes time and foresight, and Zombie TR just wants your sexy and delicious brains. One zombie is nothing. He's slow and can't use weapons, and you will *always* have the advantage because of that. Take him out.

Oh.

Unless, of course, he *does* raise a zombie army, which is totally possible, because as a human he *did* raise a human army of one thousand people for his charge up San Juan Hill. If that happens, my advice to you (and you're not going to get better advice anywhere else) is just, like . . . die. If TR's raised a zombie army, then humans are *done,* and I suggest you join the new winning Zombie team as soon as possible.

All hail President Zombie Roosevelt!

CONCLUSION

★ ★ ★

pres-i-dent

Origin: 1325–1375 < Latin prae *and* sidēns, *which translate to "king" and "of the fight-monsters," respectively.*

My ancient and nameless American Government professor had one, humble goal: to teach a bunch of college freshman how to read a newspaper. Some might consider that a noble pursuit, but I think we can all agree that it shrinks in the shadow of the objectively more ambitious goal of *How to Fight Presidents*. Readers may not be able to properly read a newspaper when they complete this book (the author, in fact, still cannot), but they now know the best way to beat Zachary Taylor in a street fight, where JFK's weaknesses are, and the terrifying secret of Grant's testicles.

Have I covered everything? No, but *How to Fight Presidents* was never meant to be the definitive guide on this subject, only a stepping stone for future research, a gateway book that would serve as a solid jumping-off point for your quest to learn about and then fight any and all presidents that might ever sass you. If you still have lingering questions about president-fighting, I strongly encourage you to visit your nearest library and local fight club.

The important thing to remember is that presidents are insane by nature and can become dangerous when threatened. If you ever happen to spot one in the wild and he (or *he*) sees you carrying this book, he will flip out and viciously attack you, charging like some kind of ferocious whirlwind of fists and flag pins. Bet you'll be thrilled you bought the book when *that* happens, and not just because of the content. One of the best things about *How to Fight Presidents* is that it doubles as a weapon; if every lesson fails you in your fight, just, like, throw it at the angry president you're facing.

Right at his face. He'll hate that.

ACKNOWLEDGMENTS

★ ★ ★

How to Fight Presidents* would probably never have been written had I not been born, and for that I guess I should thank my parents, Donna and Thomas O'Brien. Thank you for raising me to be curious enough to always challenge authority but respectful enough to always do it by reading, thinking, and writing.

Thanks to David, my brother who has always supported me (emotionally and, every so often, financially). I'd never be able to fight even someone who *wasn't* a president if I didn't know you were in my corner. Thanks to Tommy for his protection and guidance and all of the jokes he made when we were younger that I will continue to steal. Thanks to Marne and Dayna for making me laugh and for taking care of my big brothers.

Elise Leonard kept me sane during the exhausting ordeal that was this book, and also during everything else that's ever happened to me. I'm not sure I'd write anything at all if I didn't think she was going to read it.

Thank you, Joe Valenzuela, Mike Caruso, Chris Brugnola, and Mike Facchin. You are all much funnier than I am and growing up around you has completely shaped my sense of humor. Thank you to Nancy Lee and Kaitlin Large, who somehow magically always knew the exact right time to call me with a distraction when I needed a break from writing. Your Spider Sense for my need to procrastinate is uncanny.

A giant thanks goes to Winston Rowntree, my illustrator and a constant source of positivity. Winston's encouragement and support kept me moving. The strength of his illustrations inspired me to work harder every day, so the words could reach the incredibly high bar set by his images. (I almost made it.) Let's make lots of books together, please.

This book would have sat collecting e-dust on my hard drive had Ryan Holiday not introduced me to the literary agent who turned the manuscript into something worth reading. Ryan is one of the brightest guys I've ever met, and also he periodically sends me tiny hooded sweatshirts for my dog, which is another very good quality in a person.

Thank you to my hilarious super-agent, Byrd Leavell, who once described me as "a historian trapped in a comedian's body," which is the most flattering description I've received. Byrd has some of the best literary and comedic instincts I've ever seen, and I am very fortunate to be able to work with him.

Thank you, Suzanne O'Neill, and everyone else at Crown who took the manic ramblings of a presidential trivia nerd and turned them into a real-live book, with a cover and everything. I knew this book was in good hands from the very first email Suzanne wrote me, and I can't imagine *How to Fight Presidents* finding a home anywhere else.

Thank you, Tom Hawkins, my webmaster, for mastering all that web.

When I ditched work for weeks at a time to finish this book, the following people dipped into their already small reserves of free time and picked up my slack: Jason Pargin, Robert Brockway, Kristi Harrison, Adam Tod Brown, Cyriaque Lamar, Adam Ganser, Robert Evans, Abe Epperson, Breandan Carter, Cody Johnston, Randall Maynard, and all of the other creative geniuses at Cracked.com I might have forgotten. Thank you, Mandy, Billy, Stephen, Jason, Mitchell, Simon, Cody, Alison, Greg, GB, Stewart, and all of the other *actual* geniuses at Cracked.com I might have forgotten.

Thank you, Oren Katzeff, for always supporting me and this book and for buying me special edition Presidential Pez dispensers as soon as news broke that we sold the book. Whenever I eat candy out of the hole beneath James Monroe's chin, I'll think of you.

Noël Wells, Ben Joseph, Rachel Bloom, Nick Kocher, and Brian McElhaney very graciously donated their time and creative energy to help me work through some last-minute tweaks when my brain stopped functioning, and for that deserve free copies of this book. But every copy sold counts, so please buy your own instead and I'll just get you all a drink the next time we're out. Two copies means I'll get you two drinks. You see how this works.

A special thanks goes to Jack O'Brien, who isn't just the greatest boss on the planet but also one of the funniest and sharpest comedy writer-editors I've ever met. Thanks for all of your notes on the earliest version of this thing and for letting me skip work to write it, unless you didn't notice that, in which case I worked hard the whole time and frankly am due some overtime pay.

Anytime I ran out of steam and my brain was completely fried after spending twenty straight goddamn hours reading about Millard Goddamn Fillmore only to discover that there's nothing interesting about Millard Goddamn Fillmore, the following people could be counted on to drop everything and listen to me bitch about Millard Goddamn Fillmore over a late dinner or a series of drinks: Nick Mundy, Liana Maeby, Lisa Marie King, and Samantha Bowling, who was particularly good at dragging me out of my apartment and forcing me to be a social human being and not a weird president-obsessed shut-in.

Thank you to Michael Swaim, my coworker, frequent collaborator, and buddy for life. When I sent the first draft of my book proposal to Michael, his only note was "You should write this, I want to read it now." So, okay, I did that. Now you write a book.

If I had to actually list all of the wonderful things that Soren Bowie has done for me as a friend, colleague, collaborator, and supporter of *HTFP*, the page count of this book would grow by several hundred, and it seemed dishonest to have a book about president-fighting that featured more pages thanking Soren than anything else. I promise my next book will be *How to Thank Sorens*.

Thanks to the Santa Monica Public Library for not revoking my library card after my admittedly liberal interpretation of your due dates. Thank you to every president for being super crazy. Your as-yet-undiagnosed specific form of mental illness has been tremendous for my career.

I owe lots of hugs and treats to my dog, Jackson O'Brien, who bore the brunt of my panic attacks and late-night venting with the stoicism and dependability of the president for whom he was named. Thank you, Jackson, you good little guy. You're going to find this very sweet when I eventually teach you how to read.

About the Author

Daniel O'Brien is the head writer and creative director of video for Cracked.com. Since 2007, he has written over 300 articles for Cracked and is the cocreator, cowriter, and costar of the web series *Cracked: After Hours*. He coedited and cowrote *You Might Be a Zombie and Other Bad News* (a *New York Times* bestseller) and served as the senior writer for *The De-Textbook*. He's performed stand-up regularly since 2012, and his work has been featured on ComedyCentral.com, *USA Today, Forbes, Splitsider,* and a number of government watch lists that may or may not be related to this book about president-fighting. He lives in Santa Monica, California, with his dog, Jackson.